DO YOU KNOW . . .

- Seasonal affective disorder (SAD) has been recognized as a disorder only since the early 1980s, even though the "wintertime blues" have been around for centuries.
- Where you live can affect whether or not you get SAD.
- SAD has an impact not only on your mood but on your body, including worsening of PMS symptoms and substantial weight gain.
- A certain number of cloudy days in a row can be enough to produce SAD symptoms.
- Eighty percent of SAD patients are female.

FIND OUT MORE IN . . .

IF YOU THINK YOU HAVE
SEASONAL AFFECTIVE DISORDER

Look for these other Dell Guides for Mental Health

If You Think You Have Panic Disorder

If You Think You Have an Eating Disorder

If You Think You Have a Sleep Disorder

If You Think You Have Depression

A DELL MENTAL HEALTH GUIDE

If You Think You Have

SEASONAL AFFECTIVE DISORDER

Clifford A. Taylor, M.D.,
and
Robin K. Levinson

A Dell Book

Published by
Dell Publishing
a division of
Bantam Doubleday Dell Publishing Group, Inc.
1540 Broadway
New York, New York 10036

ISBN: 0–440–22542–6

Printed in the United States of America

Published simultaneously in Canada

May 1998

10 9 8 7 6 5 4 3 2 1

OPM

To my wife, Lynne, daughter, Whitney,
and son, Evan.

—Clifford A. Taylor, M.D.

To my brother, Gary Lichtenstein,
who lives in SAD territory.

—Robin K. Levinson

Acknowledgments

Thanks to . . .

The SAD sufferers who have courageously shared their stories and suggestions;

Laurie Martin, Lesley Meisoll, and Roger Granet, M.D., for their enthusiastic support during the writing of this book;

Literary agent Judith Riven for her editing and matchmaking talents.

Disclaimer

This book is written for educational purposes only and is not intended to replace the advice of a health professional. All treatment information is based on research findings current at the time the book was written. All names of Seasonal Affective Disorder patients and their family members have been changed, and some details were altered to further mask people's identities.

Contents

Foreword

People with seasonal affective disorder, or SAD, seem to fit the description of a "couch potato." Typically, symptoms include increased appetite with a craving for sweets or starchy foods, weight gain, a decrease in energy level, and apathy. All this results in an inability to start and finish tasks, a decreased attention span, and difficulty concentrating. In addition, SAD patients have a tendency to oversleep, and the quality of all that sleep is reduced. They also have a decreased sexual desire and tend to withdraw and avoid social contact. Another behavioral symptom of SAD is irritability owing to a sense of having too much to do. Feeling overwhelmed by the usual tasks of living and not knowing why produces enormous distress. Children, as well as adults, can fall victim to this syndrome. But in children, SAD typically manifests in difficulty getting up in the morning, a decreased desire to go to school, and a drop in academic performance in the winter months.

In short, SAD impairs the "drives"—those biological imperatives necessary for the health and fitness of any living organism. In animals, SAD might be described as a hibernation response, which is an "adapted depression" because it ratchets down all systems in order to preserve precious energy needed to survive through the winter. Although there are times when we, too, would like to crawl into a cave to get away from it all, our lifestyle requirements do not grant us this luxury. Instead, a SAD sufferer may crawl into bed at seven P.M. This happens to a patient of mine, a schoolteacher who starts to fall asleep right after dinner in winter. This causes him to feel extremely guilty because he cannot respond to his wife and children and remain involved in their after-dinner activities.

Seasonal affective disorder should not be confused with situational sadness, such as the holiday blues, which is psychological and stems from bad memories, loneliness, conflict, or shouldering too much responsibility. SAD, by contrast, has a physical basis and is related to a sensitivity to decreased sunlight in the winter months. Another hallmark of SAD is a palpable improvement in mood, increased energy, and diminished food cravings with the return of spring.

Some SAD sufferers are also affected whenever there are several overcast days in a row, regardless of the season. Likewise, in many work settings, people have to work long hours in windowless offices and hardly see the daylight. One of my patients must rise before sunrise in the winter and drive to work in the dark. Because of the shortened days and her long hours, it is dark again on her commute home. She rarely sees the light of day until the weekend, if the sky is not too cloudy, of course.

Fortunately, there are a number of highly effective, surprisingly inexpensive treatments for SAD, and this book covers them all—thoroughly and objectively. It is my sincere wish that the information that follows will help you transform your wintertime sadness into joy.

—Clifford A. Taylor, M.D.

Chapter One

SEASONAL AFFECTIVE DISORDER: OVERVIEW

THE SUN RETURNS

*It is the most wonderful time of year
As I count how many weeks until we change the time
To Daylight Savings.
April 6—only a week before my birthday
The Sun returns.*

*A faint hint of spring is in the air.
I hear the robins singing in the trees.
Light lingers until six-fifteen now
And soon seven P.M. will not feel
Like the isolation of three A.M.
The Sun returns.*

*I am excited for this time of year
Yet cannot break the grip that
Fall holds on my life.
The anxiety—the depression—the feeling
That I don't live in the same reality
As everyone else.*

*But, for now,
The only idea I can focus on is that for a few months
Of this year
The Sun returns.*

And for that fact, I am deeply grateful.

—Robbyn Turner, February 8, 1997

Robbyn Turner is a bright, capable communications instructor at two North Carolina universities, where she garners stellar evaluations from her students and praise from her colleagues. In graduate school, she had maintained a perfect 4.0 average. She is only thirty-three, and to those who don't know her well— and to many who do—Robbyn seems perpetually on top of her game. Yet, this mother of two spends fully half of each year feeling emotionally out of control. She grows irritable and prone to picking fights with her husband. She overeats, oversleeps, becomes anxious driving her car, and has trouble keeping up with her busy schedule. Christmas runs head-on into her annual agony.

Like an estimated 10 million Americans, or six percent of the population, Robbyn has seasonal affective disorder, a comparatively new diagnosis that, for most sufferers, makes the short, dark days of fall and winter feel like an emotional black hole. The disorder seems to be triggered by a lack of early morning sunlight, which is believed to disrupt the internal clock and alter brain chemistry in vulnerable people. Bodily rhythms such as sleep cycles, hormone secretions, and temperature fluctuations may fall out of sync. This can result in chronic lethargy, oversleeping, and a host of other symptoms. Brain chemicals, such as serotonin, that are responsible for controlling mood, may become abnormal in SAD, leading to depression, social withdrawal, irritability, and intense cravings for sweet and starchy foods, and in some cases, alcohol. Despite the emotional and behavioral upheavals, most victims fail to realize they have a diagnosable psychiatric condition. And they don't know that highly effective treatments exist to relieve their cyclical suffering.

Seasonal affective disorder is a major depressive disorder, perhaps the most pervasive mental-health problem of our time. Descriptions of the depression experience are myriad. Some of the more familiar are "a stormy cloud," "a downward spiral," "a bottomless pit," "looking at the world through gauze," "lost in a fog," "a huge weight on my shoulders," "moving in slow motion," "down in the dumps," "walking through mud," "feeling empty inside," and "trapped in sadness." When depression hits seasonally, phrases like "I hate winter," or "I'm not a winter person" become common excuses for lapses in school, work, or social settings.

If these statements ring true for you or someone you love, take heart. By opening this book, you are already on the road back to mental health. The following pages will answer many of the questions you may have about seasonal affective disorder and will provide the latest information on the various treatment options. This book may also help you decide whether you need treatment at all, for not everyone who feels "down in the dumps" has a true mental-health problem.

Seasonal affective disorder—known by its convenient acronym SAD—is a severe form of wintertime blues or doldrums. The blues, clinically referred to as "subsyndromal seasonal affective disorder," or S-SAD, strikes an estimated 25 million Americans, or 14 percent of the population, making it more than twice as prevalent as full-blown SAD. Figuring out whether you have SAD or S-SAD is the focus of Chapters Two and Three, which detail symptoms

and causes. Chapter Four will help you find the right
health-care practitioner to help you overcome your
seasonal mood disorder. Chapter Five shines a spot-
light on phototherapy and explains why exposing
yourself to intense, artificial light can be so effective.
Where to buy a quality phototherapy device and
how to use it are also discussed in Chapter Five.
Using antidepressant medication and psychotherapy
alone or in concert with phototherapy are the topics
of Chapters Six and Seven. The pros and cons of alternative depression treatments, such as St. John's
wort and acupuncture, are also covered. The final
chapters present dozens of tips and strategies aimed
at preventing seasonal depression and ways to cope
with your current or next episode of SAD or S-SAD.
Throughout this book, you will find reasons for hope.
Even as scientists toil to unravel the mysteries of SAD,
this disorder may already be the most treatable of all
the depressive illnesses.

How does it feel to have SAD?

As you will see in Chapter Two, both SAD and nonseasonal (classical) depression provoke an overwhelming sense of sadness and hopelessness. Depression
victims may feel incompetent and irritable for no apparent reason. There are, however, important differ-
ences between SAD and classical depression. While
classical depression is usually accompanied by insomnia, loss of appetite, and weight loss, most people with
SAD experience so-called atypical depressive symptoms: oversleeping, overeating, and weight gain of up
to ten pounds or more over the winter. In Chapter
Three, you will find a fascinating hibernation theory
for these phenomena.

What truly distinguishes SAD from other mood disorders, however, is its timing and cyclical nature. Often with frightening predictability, symptoms typically begin in September or October and last until April or May. Although some people experience SAD in summer, for most sufferers, seasonal depression is a frozen lake that thaws only with the coming of spring.

When was SAD first described?

The origin of SAD as a psychiatric diagnosis dates back only to the early 1980s. The first identified SAD victim was Herb Kern, a research scientist with a background in engineering. Having experienced severe mood swings for decades, Mr. Kern had noticed and documented a clear seasonal pattern to his condition. At the end of each summer, he'd begin to grow anxious. As the days grew colder and shorter, he'd begin to overeat, gain weight, sleep more than usual, and have difficulty getting his work done. By midwinter, his energy level and productivity would slip into a trough. With the onset of spring, his energy, self-confidence, and productivity returned to normal. Indeed, springtime made him almost manic, able to sleep just a few hours at a stretch. Mr. Kern suspected that his depression might be linked to a lack of sunshine in winter. He contacted the National Institute of Mental Health (NIMH) to explore his theory. There, he met research psychiatrist Norman E. Rosenthal, M.D. Dr. Rosenthal, a South African native, had experienced profound seasonal mood changes himself after moving to New York to begin his psychiatric residency training a few years earlier.

At the NIMH in Washington, D.C., Dr. Rosenthal

and his colleagues were investigating the effects of bright light on mood and activity levels in humans and animals. They suggested that Mr. Kern expose himself to three hours of intense artificial light each morning and evening. After three days of light therapy, Mr. Kern's mood was much improved. In 1984, Dr. Rosenthal and his colleagues published the first formal description of SAD in the scientific literature. Today, Dr. Rosenthal, now chief of the Section of Environmental Psychiatry at the NIMH, and his team continue to conduct pioneering research into SAD and its treatment.

Who gets SAD?

Not surprisingly, the rate of SAD in a given population depends largely on how far that population lives from the equator. People in the central and northern regions of the United States are much more likely to experience wintertime blues or depression than those in the southern areas. According to surveys, less than five percent of people living in the southern United States, from Florida to Arizona, experience depressive symptoms in winter. In northern regions, including New England, the Northern Plains, and the Pacific Northwest, at least 10 percent of the population suffers from SAD. Overall, an estimated 25 percent of the U.S. population experiences S-SAD.

"I've always envisioned myself living on a tropical island somewhere," says Joy, a Seattle, Washington, resident in her mid-twenties who believes she has suffered from SAD most of her adult life. "I hate my life during the winter months here in Seattle."

Joy, an office administrator, attained partial relief through several sessions of psychotherapy but does not wish to try light therapy or medication because she doesn't want to expose herself to anything "artificial." Robbyn Turner recently began taking Prozac and is hopeful that this antidepressant, combined with psychotherapy, will alleviate her symptoms. Another SAD patient, Joe (not his real name), a retiree living in northern New Jersey, also has manic depression. After a couple of false starts, he now successfully uses light therapy to bring himself out of a down mood. Other aspects of Joy's, Robbyn's, and Joe's stories will unfold as you progress through this book.

If you get nothing else from *If You Think You Have Seasonal Affective Disorder,* know that the misery you face in fall and winter need not be a recurring part of your life. The sooner you educate yourself about SAD and seek out treatment, the faster you will weather this storm and rid yourself of seasonal depression—perhaps forever.

Chapter Two

SYMPTOMS AND DIAGNOSIS

What is the difference between the winter blues and seasonal affective disorder?

The blues or doldrums are usually associated with mild sadness and lethargy that are noticeable but not severe enough to interfere with day-to-day functioning. For example, getting the blues can bring you down but not to the point where your negative emotions or fatigue are impairing your decision-making ability, motivation, productivity, or relationships. Wintertime blues are not generally accompanied by physical symptoms, such as intense carbohydrate cravings or chronic oversleeping (hypersomnia), which are quite common in seasonal affective disorder. For many people, the blues stem from being cold and less physically active in winter. A blue mood is not severe enough to warrant professional help. Getting the blues may even be a healthy coping mechanism in the face of a negative or stressful situation.

While some people with the blues may claim they are "depressed," they are not experiencing clinical depression, which by definition includes feelings of hopelessness, helplessness, and loss of pleasure that are difficult or impossible to ignore. There is little doubt that Joy falls into this latter category. "My work suffers because of my mood being so blue for at least six to eight months," she says. "I am not motivated."

What does "affective" mean?

"Affective" is an adjective whose root is the noun, affect. As described by Silvan S. Tomkins, Ph.D., an American psychologist, theorist, and philosopher who died in 1991, each of us has an affect system—a group of neurological mechanisms that link thoughts to feelings. "Affect," Dr. Tomkins taught, is a core "mental experience" triggered by a scene in life and displayed through facial expressions and physical arousal. Tomkins identified nine innate affects that we all share:

1. Interest (or excitement)
2. Joy (or enjoyment)
3. Surprise (or startle)
4. Distress (or anguish)
5. Fear (or terror)
6. Shame (or humiliation)
7. Anger (or rage)
8. "Dissmell" (a pulling back of the nose when something "smells" bad emotionally)
9. Disgust

Interest and joy are positive affects, surprise is a neutral affect, and the last six affects are all negative.

According to Tomkins, each affect is associated with a particular facial expression and other physical changes. Enjoyment is expressed through a smile. A response to fear or terror might include a fixed stare accompanied by sweating, trembling, and goose bumps on the skin. A fashion snob is displaying dissmell when she turns up her nose at someone who isn't wearing designer clothes.

Under normal conditions, these affects help us cope with the world. Trouble begins when our affects occur at abnormal intensities. For example, a normal dose of the fear affect helps us avoid dangerous situations; too much can lead to panic disorder. Having an excess of the excitement affect produces mania.

It is rare to experience one affect at a time. Human beings are complex creatures, forever mixing and matching affects, much like a painter combines primary colors to create different hues. Unlike the artist whose paint-mixing is a deliberate act, however, our mixing of affects is done unconsciously. The result is either normal or abnormal, depending on the circumstances and a person's psychology and biology.

Depression—seasonal or otherwise—is a combination of three negative affects: distress/anguish, fear/terror, and shame/humiliation. All are experienced for a sustained period of time, but the intensity and ratio of each affect varies from person to person. If you cry a lot during your winter depressions, you have more distress/anguish affect than someone whose depression comes out primarily as self-loathing. Self-loathing means the shame/humiliation affect is playing a larger role.

Tomkins's affect theory may help explain why certain antidepressants, such as Prozac, are useful against obsessive-compulsive disorder and anxiety as well as depression: There is an overlap of affects in all these disorders.

Is an affect the same as a feeling, emotion, or mood?

No, but all these experiences are connected through a hierarchy. Affect is the most basic experience. A feeling refers to the conscious awareness that an affect has been triggered. This is why you feel sad when you are depressed. As you remember past events that also made you feel sad, your feelings evolve into an emotion. A sustained state of emotion is called a mood. An abnormal mood suggests the presence of an unresolved conflict or a biological illness, such as depression.

How many forms of depression are there?

There are three main categories of clinical depression: bipolar disorder (manic depression), dysthymia, and major depression.

People with bipolar disorder experience episodes of clinical depression and periods of mania—an elevated, expansive, or irritable mood—each of which last more than a week. During the manic stage, thoughts race through the patient's head, and he or she may talk incessantly. Grandiosity, reduced sleep, distractibility, and poor judgment are the other hallmarks of the manic phase of bipolar disorder. Bipolar disorder, also known as manic-depressive illness, afflicts less than two percent of the U.S. population.

At some point during their lives, approximately six percent of Americans will experience dysthymia (diss-THI-me-ah), a mild, chronic depression or despondency that lasts for at least two years in adults and one year in youngsters. Dysthymia is also referred to as depressive personality, minor depression, depressive temperament, or dysthymic disorder.

Major depression, also known as major depressive

disorder or unipolar depression, does not last as long as dysthymia but tends to be more severe and disruptive to a person's life. It is also the most common form of depression, affecting 10 to 25 percent of women and five to 12 percent of men, according to epidemiological studies. Major depression has several subcategories, including depression with seasonal pattern, severe depression with psychotic features (depression plus delusions or hallucinations), major depression with melancholic features (the depressed mood fails to brighten, even briefly, when something good happens), postpartum depression (depression that begins within a year after childbirth), and adjustment disorder with depressed mood (tearfulness, sadness, or hopelessness triggered by a life change, such as going away to college or switching jobs). Another book in this series, *If You Think You Have Depression* (Dell, 1998), focuses on the diagnosis and treatment of nonseasonal forms of depressive illness.

Is depression with seasonal pattern the same as seasonal affective disorder?

Yes and no. Like the phrase "melancholic features," the phrase "seasonal pattern" is known as a "specifier" in psychiatric parlance. Specifiers are commonly used to fine tune a broader diagnosis. "Seasonal pattern" or "seasonality" can be applied to depression or other mood disorders, such as anxiety disorder and mania, if they recur seasonally. The season does not necessarily have to be winter. Since depression is the most widespread seasonal mood disorder, and since winter is the most common time for seasonal mood abnormalities to set in, SAD almost always refers to wintertime depression.

How does SAD differ from nonseasonal depressions?

As mentioned in Chapter One, the timing and cyclical nature of symptoms is what sets SAD apart from all other forms of depression. Nonseasonal (classical) depression can develop any time of year without warning, or it can emerge as a response to stress. A major depressive episode lasts about six months on average, with a range of several weeks to a year or longer. Classical depression, as well as dysthymia, can be solitary events, or they can recur throughout a person's life. In seasonal affective disorder, mood changes usually begin in fall, worsen in winter, and disappear in spring and summer.

Major depression and dysthymia typically begin in adulthood, often in the third or fourth decade of life, and may continue into the retirement years, although children are sometimes affected. Seasonal affective disorder occasionally begins in childhood but primarily plagues people during their twenties, thirties, and forties. Senior citizens can also be affected by SAD.

All forms of depression afflict females in greater numbers than males, but that statistic is particularly stark when it comes to SAD: A startling 80 percent of SAD sufferers are female. The following chapter offers possible explanations for this gender variance.

The final difference between SAD and other forms of depression is population distribution. Classical depression and dysthymia are found throughout the world at roughly equal rates. SAD is more prevalent in middle and northern latitudes, where winter conditions last longer.

What are the most common symptoms of seasonal affective disorder?

A depressed mood—feeling down in the dumps, sad, or empty—is universal in SAD. Other SAD symptoms include four or more of the following:

- Anxiety—feeling apprehensive or fearful
- Difficulty concentrating
- Irritability—being annoyed or angered easily
- Anhedonia—loss of the capacity to experience small pleasures or to derive pleasure from daily rituals; withdrawal from pleasurable activities
- Lack of motivation, initiative, and drive
- Apathy—disinterest, not caring
- Cravings, particularly for carbohydrates, often at night
- Substantial weight gain
- Decreased sex drive
- Oversleeping (hypersomnia)—four or more extra hours per day, in extreme cases
- Lethargy
- Feeling hopeless or helpless
- (In women) worsening of premenstrual symptoms

As is true with classical depression, SAD produces multiple symptoms. In general, the more symptoms you have, the more severe your disorder. However, you need not have all the symptoms listed above to be diagnosed with SAD. In some people, appetite remains normal, but they chronically oversleep and have no desire for sex. In others, SAD saps motivation and sparks cookie cravings, but sleep patterns remain normal. There are also atypical SAD symptoms, such as insomnia and appetite loss. SAD can even strike in summer. The only way to know for sure whether you have SAD is to be evaluated by a qualified mental health professional (see Chapter Four).

Are symptoms of nonseasonal depression different from SAD symptoms?

Usually. The most common symptoms reported by SAD sufferers—oversleeping, overeating, and weight gain—are considered atypical in nonseasonal major depression. What SAD and classical depression have in common are feelings of emptiness or sadness plus loss of interest or pleasure in almost everything. According to the American Psychiatric Association's *Diagnostic and Statistical Manual-Fourth Edition (DSM-IV)*, major depressive disorder (an umbrella diagnosis that includes SAD) also include four or more of the following symptoms:

- Losing or gaining more than five percent of your body weight in a month (without dieting).
- Insomnia or oversleeping.
- Visible "psychomotor agitation" (extreme nervousness) or "psychomotor retardation" (being slowed down).
- Fatigue or loss of energy.
- Feelings of worthlessness or excessive inappropriate guilt.
- Trouble thinking or concentrating, or indecisiveness.
- Recurrent thoughts about death, recurrent suicidal fantasies without a specific plan, a

specific plan for committing suicide, or an actual
suicide attempt.

Symptoms must continue every day or almost
every day for a minimum of two weeks to justify a
diagnosis of depression.

Aside from overeating and oversleeping, what other behavioral changes are associated with SAD?

People with SAD, as well as those with other depressive illnesses, are at increased risk for drug and alcohol abuse. Whether they realize it or not, depressed
patients who engage in substance abuse are trying to
blunt the emotional pain of their disease. Alcohol
may contribute to or mask depression symptoms,
or it may diminish the effectiveness of treatment.
What's more, alcohol abuse that begins during a
bout with SAD can turn into a year-round addiction,
especially if addictive illness runs in the patient's
family.

Some SAD sufferers drink several cups of coffee
or other caffeinated beverages a day in an effort to
combat their lethargy and fatigue. SAD sufferers also
tend to withdraw socially during the winter.

How can I evaluate the seriousness of my depression?

Degree of seriousness is a function of the intensity,
duration, and number of symptoms. If you have two
or three symptoms, and they don't yet interfere with
your life, then your case is considered mild. If, on the
other hand, you have had six symptoms for several

weeks, and they are growing more intense, then your case would probably meet the criteria for major depression. You would not be diagnosed with SAD unless your symptoms had a clear-cut seasonal pattern of onset and remission.

Another approach to determine the depth of your depression is to ask yourself, "To what degree is my depression adversely affecting my work, leisure time, and relationships?" or, "On a scale of zero to ten, with ten representing the best I have ever felt, how do I feel right now?" If you answer seven or eight, your depression is probably mild. Five or six might indicate a moderate degree of depression, and one to three suggests your depression is severe. Rating your own mood is hardly scientific, but it can give you a subjective sense of where you stand. Repeating this exercise once a month after you start treatment can help you gauge your progress.

In general, you may be suffering from SAD if you experience any of the following on a seasonal basis:

- Uncontrollable eating and feeling that you cannot control your weight;
- Problems waking up in the morning;
- Difficulty concentrating and thinking;
- Feeling incompetent, unworthy, bad, or unreliable;
- Difficulty completing work assignments, chores, or other tasks in a timely manner—tasks that you accomplish more easily during other times of the year;
- Feeling sad, with or without crying.

Can SAD cause psychosomatic illnesses?

Yes. In some cases, psychosomatic illness is considered "masked depression." A psychosomatic illness is any physical symptom that can be attributed to a mental, rather than a physical, cause. Psychosomatic symptoms most commonly occur among people who have trouble putting their feelings into words. Their mood disturbances are expressed through physical sensations or perceived ailments, such as headaches or stomachaches. A function of a person's psychology and physiology, psychosomatic illness affects clinically depressed men and women equally. Physical ailments being produced by SAD or another mood disorder cannot be confirmed by a physical examination or blood or urine tests. You may hear your therapist refer to psychosomatic illness as a "psychophysiological disorder."

Is the severity of SAD symptoms the same in everyone?

Not at all. As with other forms of depression, SAD symptoms manifest to different degrees in different people. At the mild end of the spectrum is subsyndromal SAD (S-SAD). Here, symptoms are considered pathological, or abnormal, but are not numerous or severe enough to significantly interfere with day-to-day functioning. For example, people with S-SAD might feel more lethargic than normal and gain a few pounds every winter. But their productivity and ability to nurture relationships are unchanged. At the other end of the spectrum are patients who are completely debilitated by their disorder. Every winter, severe SAD may lead to chronic oversleeping and frequent sick days, nightly cookie or chocolate binges, frequent family arguments, alcoholism, or suicidal thoughts.

As mentioned previously, there are also atypical cases of seasonal affective disorder. A minority of SAD patients develop depressive symptoms in summer instead of winter. Some report a decreased appetite and weight loss in winter instead of food cravings and weight gain. Insomnia (sleep disturbances), typical in nonseasonal depressions, is considered atypical in SAD patients. Oversensitivity to rejection is another atypical SAD symptom.

Every winter, I become so irritable that I want to jump out of my skin. Is this common?

Yes. Irritability is probably underreported by people with SAD because it is not generally associated with depression. When people are depressed, they often lack the capacity to respond to the demands of their environment. As a result, depressed individuals tend to be less productive at work or school. If trying to keep up with your normal responsibilities makes you irritable, you are likely to become downright angry if someone adds other tasks to your to-do list. If that someone is your boss, you will probably vent your anger indirectly, like snapping at your spouse or kids when you get home.

Says Joy: "During my SAD episodes, all I can think of is, 'How do I escape this torture?' I feel claustrophobic, like I'm going to crawl out of my skin if I don't see the sun."

Do females and males experience or express their SAD symptoms differently?

The experience is probably similar for both genders, although people's willingness to express their depression or to seek out help may be more culture-bound. Despite the male celebrities who have gone public about their depression—including Academy Award winner Rod Steiger and football player Earl Campbell—the disorder is still widely perceived as a weakness or character flaw, particularly by men. As a result, men are more likely than women to suffer in silence.

Do SAD sufferers differ in their perceptions or reactions to their symptoms?

Yes. In many respects, the psychological pain of seasonal depression is analogous to physical pain. Both can be difficult to describe in words. And everyone has a different pain threshold. Some people never donate blood because they cannot tolerate a needle in their arm. Others feel nothing when the needle is inserted. Likewise, some people can function at a remarkably high level despite their recurring dark moods. Others fall apart.

Varying sensitivities to depression become clear when you consider how severely depressed people are when they walk into a therapist's office for the first time. Some patients come in prematurely, before their sad mood reaches a clinical stage. Others have been clinically depressed for ten consecutive winters or have attempted suicide. Then there are those who seek treatment at the most appropriate moment—when their symptoms have begun to damage their quality of life.

I have premenstrual syndrome. Can SAD make my PMS symptoms worse?

There is no evidence that the biology of PMS worsens during a depressive episode. However, your perception of PMS may worsen when superimposed on the SAD phenomenon.

PMS, which affects a significant number of women during their childbearing years, produces such symptoms as fatigue, irritability, depression, water retention, headaches, and cramps. Symptoms usually occur around ovulation and remit by the time your period ends. If you are already impaired by SAD symptoms, PMS adds yet another negative stimulus, making both conditions more intolerable.

Are some races more likely than others to get SAD?

SAD is tied to latitude, not skin color. Dark-skinned populations who live in warm climates happen to experience SAD to a lesser degree because they get more sun exposure than their counterparts in temperate and colder regions.

How does SAD manifest in a child?

For many children, depression reveals itself through school-avoidance behaviors. SAD could be the culprit if your child has no social or academic problems at the beginning of the school year but begins to balk at going to school in November or December. Children may feign illness or claim they are being ignored or teased at school. It is not unusual for children with SAD to develop a genuine fear of school (school phobia). A string of rainy, cloudy days in springtime can also trigger school-avoidance behaviors in children with SAD. Because depression reduces their ability to concentrate, some children with SAD experience diminished academic performance during the winter months. In fact, SAD should be considered as a possible cause anytime a child develops school phobia for no apparent reason.

Kids with SAD also tend to be more cranky in winter, and more apathetic. They may, for example, opt to play Nintendo alone rather than go ice skating with friends.

Do senior citizens get SAD?

Yes. When SAD, or any form of depression, affects older people, symptoms may not be obvious to others. For example, a seventy-five-year-old woman who is normally sedentary may display no observable behavioral changes if she is depressed. Or family members may mistakenly attribute depressive symptoms, such as difficulty concentrating and social withdrawal, to early dementia. Stereotyping senior citizens in this manner is so common that it has a name: pseudo-dementia.

Elderly people who report seasonal mood changes should be evaluated by a mental-health specialist. Senior citizens who, for medical reasons, cannot tolerate antidepressants are often ideal candidates for light therapy (see Chapter Five).

How many SAD episodes does the average patient have before seeking help?

It varies. During initial interviews with therapists, many patients retrospectively describe SAD symptoms that have been recurring for more than a decade. Few people seek help as soon as their symptoms begin, and the majority of sufferers never seek help. It is not unusual for people to make an appointment with a therapist after seeing a report on SAD in the news media and diagnosing themselves.

Not surprisingly, fall and winter are busy seasons for therapists who treat SAD. If you think you have SAD, it would behoove you to get properly diagnosed and make a treatment plan at least a month before you expect your symptoms to set in. Hopefully, as people become more knowledgeable about SAD, they will address their problem more quickly.

Are SAD victims ever in denial of their illness?

Yes. Most people do not like to admit that they have a mental illness or emotional problem. Often, they will rationalize to justify their diminished behavior and negative outlook. They might say, "I just slow down in winter; there's nothing to do"; or "I hate going out in the cold." Or, they might misperceive winter depressions as normal.

I believe that my husband suffers from SAD but is in denial. Is there anything I can say to him without making things worse?

Yes. SAD patient Robbyn Turner, a specialist in interpersonal communications, says the situation should not be ignored. "Don't be afraid to ask that person if they're feeling okay, if they need to talk," she advises. "In a nice way, you might say, 'You don't seem like yourself lately. Is everything all right?'—and be sincere about it."

You might suggest that your husband read this book, or parts of this book, to familiarize himself with SAD symptoms and treatments. Only through open communication and education can your husband hope to overcome his problem.

What might a typical day be like during a SAD episode?

The alarm rings, but the last thing you want to do is get out of bed. The darkness of your mood matches the darkness outside your window. Your body feels heavy, as though there were weights tied to your limbs. You are lethargic. Your mouth is dry. Your senses are dulled. Your thoughts are pessimistic.

Eventually, you drag yourself out of bed, shower, and slowly get dressed. You make your way to the kitchen. Your are hungry but lack the physical and emotional energy to cook anything elaborate. You consume two pieces of toast, two cups of coffee, and a bowl of sugar-laden cereal. You avoid reading the newspaper because negative events make you cry. You have little interest in cleaning the kitchen and grow irritable as you go through the motions of getting your children ready for school. You shudder at the idea of venturing out into the cold to drive the carpool and commute to work.

When you arrive at your office, you pour yourself a third cup of coffee in an effort to feel more alert. You have difficulty concentrating and develop a headache. You avoid conversations with co-workers because you feel inadequate, ineffectual, and guilty about not doing what's expected of you. This feeds your growing sense of anxiety. You eat a chocolate bar after lunch. Your mood brightens slightly as quitting time approaches, but you can't muster the energy to go to the gym. At dinner, you consume two helpings of spaghetti and several pieces of bread. Later, you cancel plans to see friends over the weekend because you are too exhausted and depressed to socialize.

In the evening, activities that used to give you pleasure—surfing the Internet, reading a good book, helping your kids with their homework, watching a sitcom, listening to music, making love with your spouse—no longer interest you. You look forward only to eating a bag of pretzels, crawling back into bed, and shutting out the world.

The above scenario is a fairly extreme case. You may enjoy a sustained burst of pleasure or interest in something, such as a hobby. This can lull you into the false belief that your depression is ending—until you wake up feeling tired and lousy again the next day. Depression symptoms do not follow a smooth curve.

How long does an episode of SAD last?

Depending in part on how far north you live, SAD episodes usually last five to seven months, usually falling between October and May. Severity of symptoms may wax and wane, but they persist every day or almost every day throughout the episode. Depression lifts in spring and summer.

I was depressed for the first time last winter. Am I destined to get depressed every winter from now on?

No. You may have experienced a major depressive episode that just happened to occur during the wintertime. There are other possibilities. You may have had a medical illness that produced depression, or perhaps you took a medication that made you depressed (see Chapter Three). Before a diagnosis of SAD can be made, your symptoms must be clear-cut and recurrent over at least two winters, and not attributable to illness or a drug side effect or interaction. In addition, the primary trigger of your depression must be light deprivation, as opposed to other triggers, such as divorce, loss of a job, or eroded self-esteem. On average, SAD patients suffer through some nine years of wintertime depression before seeking treatment.

Do SAD symptoms come on gradually, or do they hit all at once?

The onset of depressive symptoms is usually insidious. Unless you are paying very close attention to your mood, you may not realize you are depressed until your symptoms are severe enough to hinder your daily activities. At that point, you may feel overwhelmed by fatigue, carbohydrate cravings, and a sustained feeling of sadness or emptiness. For many people, SAD is most noticeable right after daylight saving time reverts back to standard time—when you begin driving to and from work in the dark.

Does the severity of SAD symptoms change from morning to night?

Severely depressed people usually feel worse in the morning than they do during the day or at night. They may wake up feeling hopeless and anxious—as though a heavy weight is on their shoulders. These sensations generally grow less intense as the day wears on. In lesser depressions, the converse is usually true.

Must depression occur in successive winters to be diagnosed as SAD?

Yes. Depression must occur at least two consecutive winters and be separated by nondepressed periods during the spring and summer months in order to meet the criteria for a SAD diagnosis. However, SAD occasionally skips a season.

How is SAD diagnosed?

A SAD diagnosis is based primarily on the patient's history. Here is part of an interview that might take place during an initial consultation with a psychiatrist:

Doctor: What concerns do you have, and how can I help you?

Patient: I typically do well until late fall or early winter, and I've noticed a pattern. I've always hated winters.

D: Why?

P: It's cold, and I hate when I go outside in the morning and it's still dark, and then I drive home from work in the dark. I feel like I'm not getting enough sunlight.

D: Do you feel your mood has more do with the weather, or the holidays?

P: No, it's the whole thing.

D: Do you feel as though the lack of sunlight may have something to do with how you feel?

P: Yes, but it's the weather, the temperature, too.

D: Have you ever heard of seasonal affective disorder? (The psychiatrist describes SAD.)

P: Yes. I bet this is what's happening to me. It's like cabin fever, right?

D: Right. Have you ever experienced some comparable but shorter-lived symptoms when there is a long period of overcast weather?

P: Yes, I have . . .

The psychiatrist then asks the patient about her family history—whether her mother or father was more grumpy or irritable in the wintertime. Not everyone with SAD has a discernible family history of the disorder; SAD may also skip a generation.

The patient is also asked about her drinking habits and whether she takes recreational drugs.

Not everyone with SAD notices that their mood changes fit a pattern. Because depression lifts spontaneously in the spring, they may forget about their illness—until the next winter. This selective "amnesia" is why your therapist may ask to speak to your significant other.

How can my partner or spouse aid in my diagnosis?

You may be exhibiting behavioral changes that you forgot to tell your therapist about or haven't noticed. Sometimes, spouses are in a better position to observe their mate's diminished libido, altered eating patterns, changing sleep patterns, or tendency to neglect household responsibilities. Likewise, your spouse is in a good position to observe any increased alcohol consumption or eating binges. He might also have noticed that you are upset by your overall lack of productivity.

Bringing your significant other to your first appointment can make the consultation less threatening for you even as it helps the therapist diagnose your problem.

Can SAD overlap with other forms of depression?

Yes. Some people have classical depression, bipolar disorder, or dysthymia that is exacerbated in fall and winter.

How do patients generally react when they are told that they have seasonal affective disorder?

Most people are relieved to learn that there are biological and environmental factors behind their depressions. They also tend to be less ashamed and embarrassed about their diagnosis compared to people diagnosed with classical depression. Clichés such as cabin fever and wintertime blahs—even when they are severe enough to constitute a mental illness—lend a veneer of normalcy to a SAD diagnosis.

Can the therapist tell from my facial expressions or demeanor whether I am depressed?

Yes. Some depressed individuals are very withdrawn; they sit in the therapist's office like a lump of clay. Others are visibly agitated and can't seem to sit still. They may pace around the room. A furrowed brow or a flat or downward expression are other indicators of depression, as is crying. Some patients would like to cry but cannot because they are too cut off from their feelings. Two of Dr. Tomkins's three depression affects—distress and shame—mirror some of these clinical observations. Distress evokes the crying response, shame is expressed through the lowering of the head and eyes.

How can I help my doctor arrive at an accurate diagnosis?

If your mood changes happen to coincide with your move to Seattle from San Diego, that is certainly worth mentioning. If possible, investigate your family history of SAD, depression, and alcohol abuse, and report what you know to your doctor. As pointed out previously, bringing your spouse to your initial consultation can be instrumental in arriving at a correct diagnosis. If you have kept a journal over two or more years, comparing the tenor of wintertime entries to summertime entries might uncover a pattern.

Be sure to give your psychiatrist a complete list of any and all prescription and over-the-counter drugs you take. (Drugs that can produce depression as a side effect are discussed in the next chapter.) And be candid in regards to your use of alcohol and recreational drugs. Unless your life is in imminent danger, everything you say to your therapist is treated as confidential.

I visited a psychiatrist who said I didn't have SAD. I disagree. Should I find another doctor?

You are always free to get a second opinion. If two or more therapists reach the same conclusion, however, it is fair to assume they are on the right track.

Are any blood tests needed to diagnose SAD?

There are no tests that directly screen people for SAD, but there are blood tests to rule out medical illnesses that can produce depressive symptoms. You will not need blood work if your SAD is clear-cut and uncomplicated by other mental or physical disorders.

Under what circumstances might my doctor order blood tests?

If he or she suspects that a medical illness may be causing your depressive symptoms. Also, blood tests may be ordered if your depression doesn't exactly fit a seasonal pattern, or if you are experiencing your first bout with severe depression. Blood tests may include:

- Complete blood count (CBC), which tests for anemia.
- "Chem screen" to assess liver and kidney function.
- "Electrolytes" (part of the chem screen) to measure the levels of potassium, sodium, and calcium in your blood. This may rule out various metabolic causes of depression.
- "Thyroid profile," particularly a thyroid stimulating hormone (TSH) test, which can detect an underactive or overactive thyroid gland.

Depending on where you live, your blood may also be tested for exposure to Lyme disease, a tick-borne illness that sometimes causes psychiatric symptoms, especially depression. Lyme disease is most prevalent in the northeastern United States but has also been reported in other regions and other countries.

Do clinicians ever misdiagnose SAD?

SAD may, at times, be diagnosed inappropriately in a patient who has a relatively complex depression or whose depression stems from a medical problem or drug interaction. If your therapist is inexperienced, your depression may be presumed to be a seasonal phenomenon when it is not.

Conversely, seasonal depression may be written off as stress over final exams, work deadlines, or the holidays. SAD may also be missed because symptoms

coincide with social isolation that happens naturally
in colder weather and when the luster of a new
school semester has dulled.

**SAD symptoms seem simple enough to identify. Why
shouldn't I diagnose myself, buy a light box, and
avoid the trouble and expense of seeing a specialist?**

While it is possible to correctly diagnose yourself,
it is extremely important to get confirmation from
a mental health expert. In the absence of this confirmation, self-diagnosis can be dangerous. Your
depression may be caused by a drug you are taking,
or it could signal a serious medical condition such
as Parkinson's disease, multiple sclerosis, or thyroid dysfunction. You may also have undiagnosed
dysthymia, bipolar disorder (manic depression), or
another psychiatric problem, and SAD is only
adding to your misery. If you have bipolar disorder, using light therapy at the wrong time of day
can induce mania. Inappropriate administration
of light therapy can also produce agitation and
insomnia, which may further destabilize your
mood. Paying for professional advice clearly is
money well spent.

It may also interest you to know that the cost of
diagnosis and treatment for SAD is generally lower
than it is for many other psychiatric disorders.
Most SAD patients need only an initial consultation
plus one or two therapy sessions to develop and
fine tune an appropriate treatment protocol. If
treatment goes well, all you may need next fall is a
telephone conversation with your therapist to reini-
tiate light therapy or to renew an antidepressant
prescription.

Seeing a therapist can also save you money in the long run. For example, no insurer would even consider reimbursing you for a light box without a written diagnosis and treatment recommendation from a licensed health-care provider.

Chapter Three

WHAT CAUSES
SAD?

**I always feel sad, anxious, tired, and stressed out
around Thanksgiving and Christmas. Do I
have SAD?**

If your mood returns to normal by New Year's Day,
it is unlikely that you are suffering from seasonal affective disorder. SAD usually lasts five months or
longer, while the holiday blues last a few weeks, at
most. According to SAD researcher Dr. Rosenthal,
there is no evidence that holiday stress is involved in
winter depressions. Holiday stress may, however,
"aggravate the depressing effects of light deprivation," Dr. Rosenthal notes in a 1993 report that ap-
peared in the respected *Journal of the American
Medical Association.*

Holiday blues are extremely common—and quite
normal, given the extraordinary pressures on your
time and pocketbook. Family strife, which often
comes to a head during the holidays, may be another
source of your negative mood. One way to cope is
letting friends or relatives take charge of the holiday
festivities, or hosting a pot-luck Thanksgiving or
Christmas dinner instead of doing all the cooking
yourself. If finances are tight, consider homemade
presents or less tangible gifts, such as breakfast in

bed for your spouse every Sunday for a month, or doing someone else's chores for a week.

What causes seasonal affective disorder?

There doesn't seem to be a single, overarching theory to explain all cases of SAD. For the majority of patients, however, the chief precipitant appears to be changes in light cues. Certain physiological rhythms are synchronized to cycles of day and night. As the days shorten in late fall and winter, there is a subtle shift in the body's "internal clock" to compensate. Earlier sunrises and later sunsets in spring and summer cause the rhythms to shift back into spring and summer mode.

Whether depression sets in as a result of seasonal light changes depends on a variety of factors, such as your brain chemistry, hormones, sleep habits, genes, and the way light impulses are transmitted to your brain. In certain people, evolutionary vestiges of the hibernation response also appear to play a role in SAD.

What is an internal clock?

The internal clock refers to biological rhythms. Circadian rhythms help us adapt to daily cycles of light and dark. For example, body temperature and hormonal output fluctuate on a cycle of roughly twenty-four hours. These fluctuations induce phases of alertness and activity that alternate with phases of withdrawal and sleep.

There is another internal clock, this one tied to seasonal rhythms. Shortening or lengthening photoperiods—that portion of the day when the sun is out—are tracked by our brains so our bodies "know" what time of year it is. Similarly, changes in light cues probably tell birds when to fly south and bears when to hibernate. Fertility in many animals is also regulated by an internal clock. A species is more likely to survive if its offspring are born in spring when the weather is inviting and food is plentiful.

Is SAD caused by abnormal circadian rhythms?

No one knows for sure. Some theorists say that in SAD, the circadian rhythms are delayed; the brain thinks it is later in the day than it really is, and the body responds accordingly. This so-called "phase shift delay" would help explain why SAD patients are so tired in the morning. The theory also holds that people with classical (nonseasonal) depression have a "phase shift advance"; their circadian rhythms trick the brain into thinking it is earlier than it actually is. That would account for the early-morning wakening and insomnia. In both seasonal and nonseasonal mood disorders, the brain is receiving the wrong message in regard to time.

Is SAD a biological or a psychological disorder?

Research strongly suggests that SAD is a biological disorder, though it often has psychological and social consequences. SAD symptoms can be exacerbated by psychological forces, such as low self-esteem owing, for example, to a difficult childhood or obesity.

How do changes in light cues affect the mood in people with SAD?

In theory, the brain is accustomed to cues from morning sunlight to determine where it is in the course of the day and year. When morning light hits the retina, it sends a message to the brain that it is time to wake up. In winter, particularly in northern latitudes, morning darkness tells your brain it is time to stay in bed. After the sun sets, the brain is cued to start winding down in preparation for sleep. If the sun sets at five P.M. instead of seven P.M., the desire to sleep can kick in early. This is why SAD is sometimes interpreted as a "sleep-phase shift disorder."

Conversely, early morning light exposure makes some people more energetic than normal. Some people experience a mild manic state called hypomania in the spring and summer. Recurrent mania in spring or summer is also considered a form of seasonal affective disorder.

I work in an office, exercise in a gym, and spend relatively little time outside. How can my mood be so dependent on outdoor light conditions?

You may be underestimating the amount of natural light you get each day. On your drive to work, light streams in through the car windows and reflects off the hood into your eyes. If you commute by train or bus, you're exposed to outdoor light while walking to the train station or bus stop. Sunlight also reaches you through the window of the train or bus. Even while bundled up in a parka, hat, and gloves, light continues to enter your eyes—and this is what cues your brain and internal clock. On overcast days, the intensity of outdoor light still exceeds the light level in the average home or office.

Indoors, the ambient light is generally brighter in summer than in winter. Vulnerability to SAD or S-SAD may be why some people request window offices with southern or southeasterly exposures—which receive the most light. Likewise, real estate brokers often use "sun-splashed room" as a selling point for apartments and condos.

For many people, twenty minutes of incidental exposure to outdoor light may be all it takes to keep their biorhythms in sync with the time of day and the season.

Which hormones are involved in SAD?

The only confirmed hormonal connection in SAD involves cortisol. Released by the adrenal glands, which sit on top of the kidneys, cortisol prepares us to face normal, everyday stresses. Cortisol is therefore sometimes referred to as the stress-management hormone. (The adrenals also secrete adrenaline, the fight-or-flight hormone that is released in response to extraordinary stress.)

Normally, a peak in the release of cortisol occurs around four A.M. After four, the level of cortisol in the blood gradually rises until it is time to wake up and get out of bed. Thanks to this cortisol spurt, we are prepared for the physical and mental demands of our morning routine.

In biological depressions, such as SAD, the regulation of cortisol release may be faulty. The brain, which controls all hormonal output, is probably sending aberrant signals down to the adrenals, telling the glands that something is wrong with their capacity to function. This results in high levels of cortisol being released all the time, keeping depressed people in a continually stressed state. Also, with no cortisol spurt at four A.M. to "power up" the sleeping body for the morning, people with SAD wake up feeling somewhat vulnerable and not quite on top of things. When depression is adequately treated, studies have shown that cortisol levels return to normal. Cortisol levels can be used to document the presence of SAD and other biological depressions.

How are abnormal cortisol levels detected?

This is done through the dexamethasone suppression test, or DST. To administer the test, another hormone, dexamethasone, is injected into the bloodstream. Blood levels of cortisol are measured before and after the injection. Under normal circumstances, dexamethasone forces down cortisol production. If the cortisol level is constantly high, the cortisol level remains unchanged after the dexamethasone injection.

The DST is used very selectively in SAD patients because seasonal depression is diagnosable through less expensive means (see Chapter Two). The DST is used primarily by researchers to document that a depression treatment worked.

Does melatonin play a role in SAD?

Melatonin's role—if any—in SAD is not understood, although recent research findings suggest several possibilities. For example, scientists have discovered that production of melatonin—a hormone associated with sleep—is turned on in the dark and inhibited by light. At least one study found that people with abnormally elevated blood levels of melatonin during the day may be vulnerable to SAD. When SAD victims' daytime melatonin levels declined, so did their cravings for carbohydrates. Other research suggests that melatonin helps control human responses to seasonal changes. For example, melatonin may affect a person's energy level, appetite, and sex drive, all of which can be altered during a depressive episode.

There is another possible connection. Melatonin is manufactured from serotonin in the pineal gland. Serotonin is a neurotransmitter (brain chemical) that helps regulate mood. Biological depressions are associated with an insufficient amount of serotonin being made available to certain brain cells, or neurons. It may be that a melatonin imbalance triggers abnormalities with serotonin or other brain chemicals, resulting in depression.

If SAD is caused by diminished light, why aren't all blind people depressed?

There have been no detailed investigations that answer this question. Studies have shown that when sighted people are exposed to steady light levels over an extended period of time, their circadian rhythms free-run on an average cycle of about twenty-five hours. Melatonin production in some blind people follows a similar cycle, research has shown. It may be that blind people have made some type of chronic adaptation to keep their internal clocks on a regular schedule. Also, many blind people can sense light and dark. This may be sufficient to signal the brain to modulate circadian rhythms even though the person lacks the capacity for full-spectrum vision.

What causes SAD sufferers to oversleep?

There are several possible explanations. One theory is the hibernation response. In most people, this evolutionary vestige is switched off. But in some people, it seems to be switched on. This apparently happens at random across the population. If winter kicks a person into "hibernation mode," his metabolism slows down, as does his drive and energy level. The desire for sleep can be overwhelming.

Psychologically, morning darkness coupled with cold, often inclement weather makes people want to sleep late. If your work or school schedule or crying baby requires you to wake up early, it can certainly adversely affect your mood.

SAD sufferers are also prone to "sedative sleeping"—sleeping to escape reality, not because your body needs rest. If you are feeling down in the dumps, inept, hopeless, and antisocial, going to sleep is a way to avoid facing your problems. To maintain health, the average person needs six to eight hours of sleep during each twenty-four-hour period. People instinctively believe that more sleep will make them feel better. In fact, sleeping more hours than you need can make you feel worse—more depressed and more fatigued.

The notion that oversleeping causes or exacerbates depression makes better sense when you consider that sleep deprivation can be used as a short-term treatment for depression. If you are depressed and sleep half as many hours as normal for two consecutive nights, you'll often get a transient feeling of being high, which temporarily lifts depression. So, for people with SAD, it's a vicious cycle: They want to oversleep to fight fatigue and to escape from the world, but too much sleep exacerbates depression.

In Chapter Nine, you will learn about sleep hygiene

and why it is so important for SAD sufferers to adopt a disciplined sleep schedule.

What causes SAD patients to crave carbohydrates and overeat?

Again, the hibernation theory offers one possible explanation. People with SAD crave sweets and starches in order to "fatten up" for the winter.

Also, the same conscious forces at work in sedative sleeping may trigger sedative eating in certain people with SAD. Sedative eating is consuming food in an effort to reduce negative feelings, not because you are hungry. Take, for example, the woman who eats a stack of Oreos at eleven one winter night in hopes of achieving the joy affect. Instead, she ends up feeling disgusted with her behavior. This further whittles away her self-esteem, which was already suffering as a result of her seasonal depression. Yet another vicious cycle emerges.

How long does it generally take for SAD symptoms to appear?

Sudden onset of SAD is very rare. In most cases, symptoms build slowly and progressively over a course of several weeks, as minutes are gradually shaved from the daily light cycle. Often, this gradual onset goes unnoticed until the number and severity of symptoms reach a critical mass. Some people can actually predict when they will begin to feel most symptomatic. If that happens around Thanksgiving every year, it is logical to assume that low-grade symptoms are present two or three weeks earlier.

Why do people in northern latitudes suffer from SAD in greater numbers than those in southerly regions?

In northern latitudes, the photoperiod (dawn until dusk) grows shorter faster, and winter conditions last longer. This puts a more intense, collective strain on the SAD sufferer's ability to concentrate and think. For example, in the New York metropolitan area, about four months of shortened photoperiods alternate with about eight months of longer days. In northern Canada, winter light conditions last about six months. This increases the risk for SAD because there are only six months of long photoperiods to recover before winter comes around again.

Can cloudy days be dark enough to produce SAD symptoms?

Yes. Certain people's moods are very reactive to just two or three days of cloudy, rainy weather, even when they occur in spring or summer. Some people claim that a single overcast day can bring them down emotionally. Unfortunately, it is difficult to document whether such a reaction is a negative placebo effect or a genuine physiologic experience. If your mood darkens when skies are overcast, the odds are very high that you have SAD or will develop it in the future.

Can stress trigger SAD symptoms?

No, although stress can make existing depressive symptoms more difficult to cope with.

Are there any personality traits or psychological factors that make someone vulnerable to SAD?

No. There is nothing in the medical literature indicating that personality or psychology has anything to do with people's SAD risk. The disorder seems to be distributed randomly among all personality types.

Are people with nonseasonal major depression at higher risk for SAD?

While the two disorders can overlap, there is no statistical correlation between seasonal and nonseasonal depressions. That may not be true for people with bipolar disorder. SAD researcher Dr. Rosenthal has found a preponderance of women with bipolar disorder who are more prone to depressive phases in winter and manic phases in summer. At least one man with bipolar disorder, Joe, has a similar experience. "I've been seeing the same psychiatrist for years, and when we plotted my ups and downs, the downs were far greater in the darker months of the year," he says.

Why are 80 percent of SAD patients female?

There are no known biological reasons for this gender variance. It may be that SAD strikes men and women equally, but women are more likely to report their depression and seek help. And help can be easier to find if you are a woman. Because they bear children, most women are already plugged in to the health-care system. Should a woman need mental-health services, she can ask her gynecologist for a referral.

Additionally, women tend to be more tuned in to

their emotional states. Because they expect to receive support and empathy from peers, they may feel more comfortable talking about their problem and less stigmatized by their depression. Many men, on the other hand, perceive depression as a weakness. They may falsely assume that peers will criticize them or take advantage of them if they disclose that they suffer from seasonal mood changes. Instead of obtaining help, many men suffer in silence.

Does SAD have a genetic basis?

Because SAD is a relatively new diagnosis, there have been no systematic studies investigating whether this disorder is passed from one generation to the next. However, it is well established that nonseasonal depression and bipolar disorder do run in families. It is therefore possible that certain groups of SAD sufferers have a genetic predisposition for seasonal mood changes.

"I predict that the area of genetics will offer very significant breakthroughs in our understanding of the biological basis and in our treatment of SAD in the future," notes Dr. Rosenthal.

Can eye problems predispose someone to SAD?

Some people have a condition called reduced retinal light sensitivity, referring to an impairment in the retina's ability to respond to light and send signals back to a part of the brain called the hypothalamus. The retina is the back portion of the eye that is connected to the optic nerve. The hypothalamus controls a number of core bodily functions, including body temperature, appetite, sex drive, and, to some degree, metabolic rate and energy level. So, presumably, if there is less light traveling from the eye to the hypothalamus, it may prevent the hypothalamus from being as vitally stimulated as it ordinarily is. The functions controlled by the hypothalamus may be diminished as a result. The problem could lie in the retina itself or somewhere along the pathway between the eye and the brain. Reduced retinal light sensitivity may be harmless in spring and summer but may cause difficulty in winter when there is less light available to stimulate the hypothalamus.

Are night-shift workers more likely than day workers to develop SAD?

No, as long as the workers keep a steady nighttime work schedule. People on rotating work shifts may be more prone to depression owing to disturbances in circadian rhythms and other biological processes.

Which medications can cause depression as a side effect?

Technically, any medication that crosses the blood-brain barrier—the mysterious area of the brain where some drugs get through and others don't—has the potential of causing depression. Of course, some drugs are more notorious than others. Valium, sleeping pills, and other tranquilizers and anti-anxiety drugs may mask depression, especially with long-term use. Certain antibiotics can cause depression, as well. Aldomet, used to treat high blood pressure, is also known to cause depression. In fact, almost all antihypertensives except calcium channel blockers can cause depression. The worst are probably the beta blockers, a class of blood pressure–lowering drugs, which can cause significant depression. Recent findings have shown that beta blockers may also impair the production of melatonin, which can contribute to problems with the body's biological and circadian rhythms.

What should I do if I must take one of these drugs to maintain my health?

If you are prone to seasonal depression, inform your doctor before beginning a new medication, particularly if you'll be taking it in fall or winter. It may be possible to substitute another drug. If there is no way around your dilemma, it is safe to take an antidepressant to treat a drug-induced depression. However, taking an antidepressant under these circumstances should always be a last resort.

Conversely, if you are depressed and taking medication to control a medical problem, tell your psychiatrist. It may be that your depression is being caused by the drug and not by SAD. Give your doctor the name of any and all prescription and over-the-counter medications you are taking. It is possible that your depression is a result of a drug interaction and can be corrected by a medication switch.

Chapter Four
FINDING HELP

What motivates SAD sufferers to get help?

Most SAD patients make their first appointment after learning about SAD in the news media or speaking with someone who is being treated for SAD. It is not unusual for these patients to diagnose themselves prior to their initial consultation. Wisely, they want confirmation of their self-diagnosis.

Of those patients who never heard of SAD, most seek help because they are fed up with their recurring bouts of depression. They are frustrated by their lack of productivity at work, home, or school every winter. In some cases, they are facing possible unemployment or divorce as a result of their recurring problem. Occasionally, someone attempts suicide or otherwise hits bottom before realizing that he or she needs professional help.

Unfortunately, many SAD sufferers never get help; they resign themselves to wintertime depression, they forget about their symptoms as soon as spring comes, or they live in denial that anything is wrong.

Who is best qualified to diagnose and treat SAD?

Psychiatrists may be best suited to identify SAD patients and help them recover, although many psychologists and clinical social workers are also skilled in SAD diagnosis and treatment. In addition, some internists and obstetrician-gynecologists (ob-gyns) have special training in depressive illnesses, including SAD.

Because they have a medical degree, psychiatrists can perform a physical exam and, if necessary, order blood tests designed to rule out illnesses that can cause depression. Internists can do the same, but they don't usually offer psychotherapy, as psychiatrists do, and internists are not necessarily experts in the administration of psychotropic (mood-altering) medications. While many psychiatrists, psychologists, social workers, and psychiatric nurses are familiar with phototherapy technology, psychiatrists are the only mental-health professionals who (at this writing) can prescribe antidepressants. That option becomes important if light therapy is unsuccessful or inadequate, or if you have other psychiatric problems in addition to SAD.

Can my family doctor help me?

Perhaps. Some, but not all, primary care physicians are comfortable treating SAD. Research has shown that all psychiatric diagnoses, including depression, are underdiagnosed and undertreated by primary care doctors, including internists, family practitioners, ob-gyns, and pediatricians. To combat this problem, the psychiatric community has launched a major effort to train front-line doctors in how to recognize all forms of depression in their patients. In cases where SAD is diagnosed, psychiatrists are encouraging these clinicians to treat uncomplicated cases with light therapy or medication and brief counseling, and to refer complicated cases to a mental-health specialist.

Drug companies are also trying to persuade more primary care physicians to treat depression. For example, antidepressants are heavily advertised in generalized medical journals, such as the *Journal of the American Medical Association*, whose readership includes primary care physicians.

Patients should not expect family doctors to provide psychotherapy beyond some arm-around-the-shoulder emotional support. And the doctors ought to know when they are in over their heads. If a patient is becoming suicidal or is abusing alcohol or drugs while depressed, for example, a referral should be made to a mental-health specialist.

I'm sure I had SAD symptoms during my annual physical last year, but my internist didn't pick up on them. Why?

Considering the huge number of symptoms, illnesses, diagnostic tests, and medications that internists need to know about, it is probably unrealistic to expect them to have expertise in SAD or other depressive disorders. This is unfortunate because as many as 30 or 40 percent of people who see physicians because of medical complaints actually have a primary psychiatric disorder of depression or anxiety, which is producing real or imagined physical symptoms. SAD patients may complain about vague stomachaches or headaches. They may tell their doctor they've lost their "edge," that they feel overtired, that they are hungry all the time. As Chapter Two pointed out, SAD symptoms vary from patient to patient. The diagnosis is sometimes hard to recognize, even by a mental-health expert.

I can barely drag myself out of bed. How can I be expected to motivate myself enough to see a therapist?

Everyone has an observing ego—the part of your psyche that can take a step back and look at things objectively, if only for a short while. To do this, you must try to separate your intellect from your emotional state. Ask yourself: "Is it reasonable for me to get help?" Even if your emotions say, "No," try to follow your intellect, which may be saying, "Yes."

If you cannot use your observing ego, lean on people who love you. Ask them to read this chapter and find you a therapist. You can always turn to a rabbi, priest, or minister for guidance.

What are the possible consequences of not getting professional help for my depression?

In a worst-case scenario, you could kill yourself. You could also put yourself at emotional risk as your view of yourself, the world, and relationships gets more and more negative. If your concentration is off and you stop caring when you have SAD, driving a car can become dangerous to you and to others. By avoiding treatment, you place yourself at risk for drug or alcohol abuse in an attempt to alter or numb your feelings.

Physically, there is a demonstrated link between depression and overall health. Depression is associated with the blunting of the immune system, which makes depressed people more vulnerable to cold germs and other infections that run rampant in winter. One study of more than 2,400 men in Finland suggests that a pervasive sense of hopelessness is a risk factor for heart disease, cancer, and other serious medical conditions. Another study found that the risk of dying from stroke was 50 percent higher among adults with severe depressive symptoms. Susan Everson, of the California Department of Health, senior author of a twenty-nine-year study, told *USA Today* that depression alters blood platelet activity in a way that could promote stroke-triggering clots.

How can I tell if my depression is severe enough to warrant professional help?

If, after reading the previous chapters, you are still unsure whether you meet the criteria for seasonal affective disorder, ask yourself the following questions:

1. Do I feel an overwhelming and prolonged sense of helplessness, hopelessness, or sadness that hits every winter and goes away in spring and summer?
2. Am I finding it difficult to perform normal activities, such as concentrating on work assignments in fall and winter?
3. Do I worry all the time or expect the worst, or am I irritable or on edge, in the fall and winter?
4. Am I doing things that are potentially harmful when I feel depressed? Am I drinking too much alcohol, abusing drugs, or am I unusually argumentative or aggressive?
5. Do I feel like my old self again—much happier and markedly more energetic—when springtime comes?

If you answer yes to any of these questions, you should strongly consider getting professional help.

How much do psychiatrists charge?

Fees vary widely, but most psychiatrists charge up to $300 for an initial consultation and $125 to $250 for a forty-five- to fifty-minute therapy session. (Fees in major metropolitan areas are generally higher than in the Midwest and rural areas.) Psychologists charge slightly less. Some practitioners and mental-health centers offer sliding-scale fees to qualifying patients with no insurance coverage. Some practitioners offer thirty-minute half-sessions or medication sessions for about $100 or less.

Fortunately, protracted psychotherapy is usually unnecessary for people with SAD. A diagnosis can often be made during an initial consultation. After that, you may only need two or three more sessions to launch and fine tune your treatment plan.

What kind of training do psychiatrists get?

Psychiatrists are medical doctors and thus have an M.D. after their name. After graduating from college, they must graduate from an accredited four-year medical school and complete four years of residency training in psychiatry. In the first year, the training is in general psychiatry as well as pediatrics, internal medicine, and neurology (the brain and nervous system). Later, psychiatric residents train more thoroughly in outpatient and inpatient settings, learning about drug interventions, electroconvulsive therapy, and different modalities of psychotherapy, behavior therapy, family and marital therapy, child and adolescent therapy, and in some programs, sex therapy. Psychiatric residents also work in the emergency room doing crisis interventions, and they provide psychiatric consultations in hospital medical units, such as obstetrics and surgical wards. Like all medical doctors, psychiatrists must be licensed by the state and earn continuing education credits annually to maintain their licensure.

After completing an approved residency program, psychiatrists become eligible to apply for board certification from the American Board of Psychiatry and Neurology. Board certification, which is voluntary, is a measure of clinical competence, not excellence. The credential is earned by passing a day-long written exam that covers psychiatry and some neurology. Doctors who pass the written exam may then take oral exams. Here, the psychiatrist is observed while interviewing a psychiatric patient and then answers examiners' questions about the case. The psychiatrist also watches a video of a patient being interviewed and again answers questions. If the psychiatrist passes these oral exams, board certification is bestowed. Beyond board certification, psychiatrists can also be elected fellowship status in the American Psychiatric Association by making a "special contribution" to the field of psychiatry.

What will happen during my first appointment?

This initial consultation is basically a conversation between two people where one—the therapist—is an exceptionally good listener. This session generally lasts forty-five to seventy-five minutes, during which the therapist asks enough probing questions to obtain a fair amount of information about your mood changes and whether they are tied to the seasons. As time permits, the therapist will try to understand how your depression has affected you and those close to you.

If the psychiatrist is fairly certain that you have SAD, he or she will probably give you some literature so you can read up on your illness and its treatment. The psychiatrist may also give you a list of companies that sell light therapy devices. You may even be told how to begin treatment.

Do psychiatrists routinely prescribe an antidepressant to SAD patients?

No. Light therapy is considered the first line of treatment for most people with SAD. If light therapy fails to alleviate depressive symptoms, an antidepressant is often the next step. Light therapy or an antidepressant may or may not be coupled with psychotherapy. If psychotherapy is to be administered, some psychiatrists rarely or never prescribe antidepressants because they believe the drugs contaminate the patient's treatment. Others view antidepressants as an integral part of SAD treatment in appropriate cases. During your initial consultation, you should feel free to ask your psychiatrist about his or her prescribing philosophy. Also, if you have strong feelings about taking drugs, make that clear.

How can I tell whether a psychiatrist is keeping abreast of research into SAD and depression in general?

Perhaps the best indicator is an academic appointment (lecturer or assistant or associate professor) at a medical school. In many cases, these part-time clinical positions are unpaid. They usually require the psychiatrist to devote a minimum of three to five hours a week teaching medical students and residents and attending grand rounds—a major lecture or case conference at the hospital. This form of service and education forces the psychiatrist to remain actively involved in a profession that otherwise can be rather isolating. Another plus is being affiliated with a well-respected hospital. This provides opportunities for the psychiatrist to exchange news and ideas with colleagues.

During an initial consultation, it is perfectly legitimate for you to ask the psychiatrist about his or her hospital and medical school affiliations. Also feel free to ask how many SAD patients the doctor has treated, and how knowledgeable he or she is about phototherapy. These kinds of questions indicate that you have done your homework and are likely to play an active role in your treatment.

What kind of training do psychologists receive?

After graduation from college, psychologists spend an average of seven years in graduate education training and research before receiving a doctoral degree, according to the American Psychological Association. Psychologists have either a Ph.D. or Psy.D. after their names and are trained in counseling, psychotherapy, and psychological testing. "As part of their professional training [psychologists] must complete a supervised clinical internship in a hospital or organized health setting and at least one year of postdoctoral supervised experience before they can practice independently in any health-care arena," American Psychological Association literature states.

Like psychiatrists, psychologists must be licensed by the state or jurisdiction in which they practice. In most states, psychologists must earn continuing education credits to renew their license. Both the American Psychological Association and the American Psychiatric Association impose a code of ethics on their members. Psychologists are not medical doctors and therefore do not prescribe medication. Occasionally, psychologists work in concert with medical doctors to help patients who need both psychotherapy and medication.

Are mental-health services generally covered by health insurance?

Most health insurance plans cover at least some mental-health services, although some plans place a cap on mental-health reimbursements or limit the number of therapy sessions you can have in a given year. If you are to engage in a course of psychotherapy, call your insurer first to verify coverage, if finances are a concern. Also find out if your insurance plan covers phototherapy devices (see Chapter Five).

Where can I get a referral to a mental health practitioner?

There are a number of referral sources:

• *Your family practitioner, internist, or gynecologist.* Tell your doctor you believe you may be suffering from depression and would like a referral to a psychiatrist or psychologist who has a special interest in treating depression. If you belong to an HMO that uses a gatekeeper model of care, you will probably need a referral from your primary doctor in order to secure coverage for mental-health services.

• *Light box companies.* Most have geographic registries of psychiatrists familiar with phototherapy. A list of companies appears in Appendix A.

• *The department of psychiatry at the nearest university medical school.* The medical school or its affiliated hospital may operate a mood/affective disorder clinic. If not, solicit names of mental-health professionals in your community who specialize in the treatment of depressive illnesses.

• *Your local hospital's physician referral service.* Even if the hospital does not have a mental-health program, it may be able to give you names of psychiatrists in your community. The hospital may also provide information about the psychiatrists' schooling, training, and professional affiliations. Bear in mind that hospitals only refer to members of their own staff.

• *A private psychiatric hospital's physician-referral service or community outreach department.* Again, you will get names only of staff members, but a psychiatric hospital may be better able to refer you to someone who specializes in depression.

• *Professional organizations.* The American Psychiatric Association and the American Psychological Association can refer you to members who practice in your area. These organizations' addresses and telephone numbers appear in Appendix D.

• *Employee Assistance Programs, or EAPs.* If your workplace contracts with an EAP, you can access it directly or through your personnel or human resources department. EAPs originally were set up to help employees with substance abuse problems but are broadening their scope to provide counseling to employees with depression and certain other mental disorders. EAP providers are trained in crisis intervention and can refer you to other mental-health providers, if necessary. There are hundreds of EAP providers nationwide, and all are set up to protect employees' privacy. There is always a risk, however, that your supervisor or co-workers will find out or assume you are having a problem. In cases where a depressed employee's job performance is declining, supervisors may urge or require the employee to consult the EAP.

• *Community mental-health centers.* These tax-supported entities charge patients on a sliding scale, according to income. Your local health department, state health department, or state department of human services can direct you to your nearest community mental-health center.

• *Religiously affiliated mental-health centers, such as Jewish Family Service and Catholic Family Service.* Psychotherapy at these centers is generally administered by clinical social workers, although some centers also provide therapy with psychologists and psychiatrists.

• *Clergy.* Your rabbi, priest, or minister should be able to refer you to a reputable mental-health professional. Many clergy members have studied psychology and may be able to counsel you themselves. Clergy members who have a degree in pastoral counseling routinely counsel people who are depressed.

• *Friends or relatives who were successfully treated for depression.* If the therapist your friend or relative used practices too far away, that therapist may be

able to refer you to a colleague who works closer to
your home. Using the same therapist as your sister or
mother is not always a good idea, however. In fact,
some psychiatrists and psychologists avoid treating
members of the same family because they find it difficult to be objective. On the other hand, some mental-
health professionals routinely treat several members
of the same family who may or may not have similar
problems.

• *Self-help groups or patient-support groups.* Find a
group near your home and attend a meeting. Chances
are the members will know which therapists are best
at diagnosing and treating depression. They will also
know which therapists you'll want to avoid. A list of
self-help groups appears in Appendix C. Another
way to find these groups is through your local hospital's community outreach department.

• *Student health centers.* Most colleges and universities provide free or low-cost mental-health services
on campus.

• *Guidance counselor or school social worker.* If
these professionals cannot help a depressed high-
school student, they will know who can.

• *Magazine articles and reference books. New Jersey
Monthly* is one of many regional magazines that peri-
odically rate mental-health facilities and providers in
their readership area. A number of publishers put out
annual health-care guides that tell readers who the best
doctors are in a particular geographic region, usually a
large metropolitan area where there are thousands of
doctors to choose from. One example is the *Guide to
Good Health,* published by *Philadelphia Magazine.*

This guide includes information on mental-health services and names top-rated psychiatrists in and around Philadelphia, as well as southern and central New Jersey. Your public library may stock more comprehensive guides, such as *Best Doctors in America 1996–97*, by Steven Naifeh (Woodward/White). You may find the Midwest, Northeast, Pacific, Southeast, or American Central edition of this volume in your local library, or you can call (803) 648–0300 for referrals. Another resource is *How to Find the Best Doctors, Hospitals, and HMOs for You and Your Family*, by John J. Connolly (Castle Connolly Guide, 1994). A version of this paperback focusing on the New York metropolitan area was published in 1996.

If possible, choose a therapist who is recommended by more than one source. If you hear the same name more than once, there is a good chance that person is highly qualified.

Should I seek out someone who specializes in depression?

Depression is the common cold of mental illness. So any mental-health professional worth his or her salt should be able to treat most depressions, including SAD, so long as the practitioner has appropriate training, experience, and credentials.

For complicated cases—SAD mingled with bipolar disorder or other psychiatric or personality disorder, SAD in people with cancer or other medical syndromes, or people who haven't responded to past treatment—it makes sense to see someone who has a well-honed expertise in depression. Of course, clinicians can represent themselves as being skilled in treating SAD, even if they are not. Credentials are important but do not guarantee that a therapist is great at diagnosing and treating SAD.

To get more substantive information, ask the therapist some of the following questions:

• *What percentage of your practice is related to depression and SAD?* Almost no one treats depressed patients exclusively. It would not be unusual, however, for a mental-health professional to deal with depression in 30, 40, or even 50 percent of cases.

• *Do you teach, lecture, or write about SAD?* Has the therapist ever spoken about SAD to community groups? Does he or she teach medical students and residents about seasonal depression? Has he or she written or edited any books, chapters, or articles about SAD? Any of the above suggests cutting-edge knowledge about depression as well as a keen interest in helping SAD patients recover.

• *Have you had any special training in SAD?* This goes back to the orientation of the professional's residency or doctoral program and any subsequent training he or she may have received.

• *Are you known in the community as someone who is knowledgeable in the diagnosis and treatment of SAD?* If so, the practitioner should be able to tell you how many primary care physicians routinely consult him or her when they have a patient suspected of having seasonal affective disorder.

My choice of doctors is limited because I am in an HMO. How can I find the best mental-health professional through my managed-care network?

Very often, managed-care patients must take what they can get, and the mental-health specialist they are sent to may not necessarily be skilled at diagnosing or treating SAD. If you belong to a large HMO, there are probably several psychiatrists and psychologists in the network. You must do some legwork to find the most appropriate one for you. If your HMO gives you names but no other information, insist on knowing more about the doctors, such as how long they have been in practice and what they specialize in. Unfortunately, that is not always an easy task if you are in the throes of depression. Your concentration skills may be lacking, and low self-esteem can prevent you from being as assertive as you need to be. If you find it difficult to persevere through the process of finding help, seek out advocates, such as family members, a family physician, or clergy person who can ask questions for you.

How do I know a particular therapist is right for me?

Assuming the therapist has proper training and adequate experience, there are three other things to look out for during your initial consultation:

1. *Is the therapist really listening and trying to understand me?* The therapist should give you his or her undivided attention. That means refusing nonemergency phone calls and barring anyone from entering the room during your session.
2. *Is this person at least as smart as me?* This is an intuitive judgment call.

3. *Is this somebody I would probably enjoy sitting next to at a cocktail party?* That doesn't mean looking for a physical attraction between you and the therapist. It means deciding whether there is comfortable communication between you to facilitate a meaningful professional relationship based on empathy and compassion.

Finding a therapist you like is almost like finding a good friend. You are looking for "chemistry"—a good match between your personalities and communication styles. This assessment will be largely intuitive on your part. In general, however, look for someone who is empathic, strong, sensitive, and at least as intelligent as you are. Give credence to any negative feelings you have during your initial consultation. If, however, you have a negative reaction to three therapists in a row, the problem may lie within you.

I'm hesitant to see a therapist because of what others might think. Is there a stigma associated with SAD?

That depends on your perception. There will always be people who fear the mentally ill or view mental illness as something to be ashamed of. There are laws on the books to protect mentally ill employees, but subtle discrimination is still a threat. Fortunately, there are self-help groups and programs such as NIMH's Depression Awareness, Recognition, and Treatment (D/ART) that battle negative perceptions through public education and patient support. If you are concerned about what other people think, you need not tell anyone outside your immediate family that you are seeing a therapist or that you have SAD.

Joe, the retiree battling both SAD and manic depression, says he isn't bothered by any stigma that may exist. "I don't broadcast it, but I don't hide what the problem is, either," he says. "I'd rather seek help than worry about what people think."

Robbyn Turner, the communications professor, generally avoids discussing SAD at work. That changed one day when several students asked why she always raises the blinds in her classroom at the start of each lesson. "I told them, 'Because for those of us who experience SAD, the sun is our link during winter,' " she explains. "A few people asked what SAD was, and I gave them a brief explanation that it's winter depression due to a change in light, which causes changes in brain neurotransmitters.

"The look on some of their faces!"

Despite that initial reaction, Robbyn's disclosure apparently inspired and sensitized at least one of her students. "He did his persuasive speech on depression, being aware of symptoms, reaching out to others, etcetera," she recalls. "It was a little awkward because he found my poem on the Internet and read it for his 'attention-getter,' even though I never told him anything about the poem."

Chapter Five

LET THERE BE LIGHT: PHOTOTHERAPY

What is light therapy?

Light therapy, also called phototherapy, is a treatment that involves daily exposing the eyes to bright artificial light under specified conditions. For many people with seasonal affective disorder, daily exposure to this intense light during the fall and winter relieve or minimize such depressive symptoms as sadness, fatigue, overeating, and oversleeping. Light therapy is also used to combat jet lag and help workers on rotating shifts change their sleep patterns.

How bright is a phototherapy light?

The intensity of therapeutic light should range between 2,500 and 10,000 lux to treat SAD. This is five to twenty times greater than ordinary indoor light, which rarely exceeds 500 lux. By comparison, walking outside on a sunny afternoon might expose you to 100,000 lux of natural light. "What appears to be critical," states a brochure from the Society for Light Treatment and Biological Rhythms, "is that the level of light produced match that of visible light outdoors shortly after sunrise or before sunset."

What is "lux"?

"Lux" is unit of measure referring to the intensity of light at a particular location. Lux is measured by a calibrated light meter, the kind used by photographers. The amount of lux entering your eyes depends on the light's intensity, how close you are to the light source, and your eyes' sensitivity to light. (People with blue eyes tend to be more light sensitive than those with darkly pigmented irises.)

The term "lux" should not be confused with watt or wattage, which refers to the amount of electrical power flowing into a lightbulb. And it is not the same as lumen, which refers to the amount of light energy being emitted by a lightbulb.

What percentage of SAD patients are helped by phototherapy?

To date, there have been no large-scale, systematic studies assessing phototherapy's success rate. However, smaller studies suggest that phototherapy is effective in 60 to 80 percent of SAD cases. That is comparable to the overall success rate of antidepressants in the treatment of both SAD and nonseasonal depressions. Sometimes, people who don't respond to an initial trial of phototherapy get better after adjusting the light's intensity, changing the timing, duration, or angle of light exposure, or shortening or lengthening the distance between their eyes and the light source.

Why is phototherapy considered the first line of treatment for SAD?

There are several reasons for this:

• Side effects are minimal or nonexistent.

- Phototherapy works fast in most cases. On average, phototherapy alleviates all depressive symptoms within three or four days of daily use. By comparison, antidepressants take an average of two to four weeks to work.
- Phototherapy is relatively inexpensive. Patients incur a one-time expense of several hundred dollars to purchase a phototherapy device and can use it every winter for many years.
- Phototherapy alleviates most or all depressive symptoms and returns energy levels to normal in the majority of SAD patients who try it.
- It is painless.
- It is convenient. Phototherapy can be administered in the comfort and privacy of the patient's home.

Do I need a prescription for a light therapy device?

No, but that does not mean you should buy one without a recommendation from a licensed health-care provider. Responsible manufacturers urge all potential customers to get professional guidance on using their devices.

Can phototherapy alleviate depression that is not seasonal?

Phototherapy has not proven to demonstrate consistent therapeutic value in the treatment of nonseasonal depressions. Nor does light therapy enhance the results of drug treatment or psychotherapy in patients with nonseasonal mood disorders. Light therapy is also ineffective in SAD patients who get depressed in summer rather than winter. Probably the best treatment for those individuals is anti-depressant medication, psychotherapy, or both.

In cases where SAD is embedded in other types of major depression or biopolar disorder, light therapy may be useful, however. For example, light therapy may protect these patients from suffering a seasonal aggravation of existing depressive symptoms.

Can light therapy help people who experience wintertime blahs but who don't become clinically depressed?

Yes. Phototherapy may provide some relief for people with so-called subsyndromal, or "subclinical" symptoms of seasonal depression. As pointed out in Chapter Two, these individuals experience mild mood and behavioral changes each winter, but their symptoms are not severe enough to interfere with their lives. In these cases, phototherapy may act as a placebo to brighten the mood, rather than a catalyst for biological change.

How does phototherapy work?

The precise mechanism of action is unclear, but the most accepted theory is that light therapy resets the body's internal clock, producing a number of physiological effects. Specifically, daily rhythms of hormone secretion, body temperature fluctuations, and sleep patterns are shifted ahead. When light enters the eyes, for example, it affects the pineal gland. At night, the pineal gland excretes sleep-inducing melatonin; daylight inhibits melatonin release. Bright light exposure in the early morning may shift melatonin cycles to a summertime schedule, reducing your need for sleep and boosting your energy level.

(SAD victims may have abnormally high blood levels of melatonin at certain points during the day.)

Another theory is that bright light exposure triggers changes in the activity of mood-center neurotransmitters, most likely serotonin, in the brain.

What time of year should I begin phototherapy?

If you develop depression in winter, the best time to begin therapy is probably mid to late fall. Beginning therapy about two weeks before symptoms occur may impart a measure of protection. If you have experienced SAD for a number of years, try to recall when you usually begin to notice mood changes. Is it just before Thanksgiving? Do you begin to feel glum and lethargic around Halloween or as soon as daylight saving time ends? Whenever your symptoms become noticeable, count back two weeks. That's when you should begin using your light box or visor. This preventive approach is akin to a hay-fever sufferer using steroid nose sprays several weeks before the allergy season hits in an attempt to head off sneezing, nasal congestion, and other allergic responses. It's hard, sometimes, to remember to use light therapy when there are no symptoms. It may help to mark your calendar or keep a diary. If you're unsure when your depression usually develops, begin phototherapy a week before the resumption of standard time.

If you don't start therapy soon enough, take heart. For many SAD sufferers, light therapy can alleviate symptoms in a matter of days, even if they don't start therapy until they are in the thick of a full-blown depressive episode.

What is the best time of day for phototherapy?

For the majority of patients, phototherapy appears to be most effective when administered in the early morning, six-thirty A.M., for example, or immediately upon waking up. Morning phototherapy sessions typically occur when it is still dark outside. Some people do better with early evening phototherapy, and others find afternoon phototherapy sessions helpful. Sometimes, light therapy is most effective when administered twice a day, in the morning and early evening. One caution: If your phototherapy is administered less than two hours before bedtime, you may have difficulty falling asleep.

Can children benefit from phototherapy?

Preliminary data suggest that up to 80 percent of children with SAD between ages seven and seventeen feel better as a result of phototherapy.

Can phototherapy be harmful?

Phototherapy is generally considered safe, as long as the user stays within the light unit's recommended guidelines. A minority of users experience headaches and eye irritation or redness. Moving farther away from the light source or shortening the treatment session may reduce any physical discomfort. Using a humidifier to moisten the dry winter air may help. A few users have reported mild, transient nausea or agitation until they became acclimated to the light's intensity. Since quality phototherapy devices filter out UV rays, there should be no burning of the skin.

If overused or administered at the wrong time of day, phototherapy can induce mania or hypomania (mild manic symptoms). In these rare instances, the patient develops insomnia, restlessness, irritability, and may even become reckless. People with bipolar disorder (manic depression) in addition to SAD are most susceptible to this side effect. The importance of seeking guidance from a health professional skilled in the administration of phototherapy cannot be overemphasized.

Can looking out a window or spending time outdoors be as therapeutic as phototherapy?

Looking out a window on a bright, sunny day may help but is probably not as potent as being physically outdoors or using a light therapy device. Although plenty of sunlight may be streaming in through a window, some gets filtered out by glass panes, shades, blinds, awnings, and roof overhangs.

Peering out a window, when coupled with exposure to low-intensity therapeutic light, has been shown to be as effective as phototherapy or being outside on a sunny day. In one experiment, investigators created a light box containing eight forty-watt non-fluorescent light tubes—which is slightly brighter than normal room light but not nearly as bright as a high intensity phototherapy device. The low-intensity light box was placed next to a window, and when SAD patients looked alternatively at the box and window for a sustained period of time each day, most of their depressive symptoms were gone within a week. While this method proved equally effective as standard phototherapy, it is an unrealistic approach because it requires many consecutive sunny days—a rare occurrence in winter.

How is therapeutic light delivered?

There are two basic categories of phototherapy devices: the light box and the newer light visor. The first light boxes became widely available in the mid-1980s shortly after SAD—and the beneficial effects of light therapy—were initially described in the medical literature. Several years later, the light visor was developed and touted as a more convenient alternative to the light box. A desk lamp that functions much like a light box is also available.

Additionally, there is the dawn simulator, which may be freestanding, attached to an alarm clock, or linked to a regular incandescent light source, such as a lamp. These simulators are designed to gradually turn up the room light in the morning. Some simulators are preset for a half-hour-long dawn; others let the user control how long it takes for the light to reach full intensity, anywhere from one minute to three hours.

What does a light box look like?

Light boxes look like free-standing versions of the wall-mounted light boxes that doctors use to read X rays. Most light boxes emit full-spectrum white light through a plastic diffusing screen, which filters out most or all dangerous ultraviolet waves. Phototherapy light boxes generally weigh six to twenty pounds, are three to five inches deep and up to two feet wide, and are portable. Some are designed to be placed in floor or desk stands so they can be tilted up or down to accommodate the user's height. There are square and rectangular versions. Small desktop models are also available. The better light boxes contain high-tech fluorescent tubes that do not flicker like

overhead fluorescent tubes and do not emit magnetic
waves. High-quality light boxes also let you adjust
the intensity.

How is the light box used?

You must orient yourself so the light shines onto
your face directly and indirectly. How far you'll need
to sit from the light is determined by the light's intensity, the severity of your symptoms, and your sensitivity to light. Your therapist will help you determine
an appropriate light dose. Your light box should include instructions listing lux ratings at various distances. For example, if your light box is set at its
highest intensity, you might receive 10,000 lux from
a distance of fifteen inches, and you might receive a
therapeutic dose in fifteen to thirty minutes at that
distance. If you sat twenty-five inches away, you
would receive 5,000 lux and need a forty- to sixty-
minute session to receive the same therapeutic dose.
At thirty-five inches, the lux you receive would drop
to 2,500, and your treatment session might last two
to three hours.

How do I determine how far I need to be from my
light box and how long my phototherapy sessions
should last?

When you buy a light box, you will receive a set of
instructions, which should be reviewed with your
therapist before you begin treatment. Since every SAD
patient is unique, you may need a lower or higher
dose of light therapy to achieve the same result as another SAD patient. If you've never tried phototherapy before, your therapist may suggest starting
with a standard dose of 10,000 lux for twenty min-

utes in the morning. If you are still depressed after one week of daily phototherapy sessions, treatment parameters should be readjusted. Using light therapy takes a sense of adventurousness. It may take two or three seasons of tinkering with distance, duration, light intensity settings, and timing of sessions before figuring out a protocol that works best for you.

How long does it usually take for light therapy to alleviate symptoms?

If you are lucky enough to hit on an appropriate light dose from the start, you may notice your symptoms disappearing in less than a week—three or four days, on average. Some SAD sufferers need three or four weeks of daily phototherapy sessions before their symptoms subside. And some patients respond more fully than others.

Your sensitivity to light, the number and severity of symptoms, and your ability to adhere to your treatment protocol all play a role in how fast you will respond. It may take some trial and error before you and your doctor can determine the optimal dose for you. Bear in mind that some SAD patients simply do not respond to light therapy, no matter how compliant they are with their doctor's orders. A good rule of thumb is to use phototherapy in various ways for a month before deciding whether to abandon it.

Should I stare into the light?

That is not necessary or recommended, as long as the light box is angled toward your face. Light reflecting into your eyes is sufficient to produce a therapeutic effect. Staring directly into a light box can cause

eyestrain, or even eye damage. Glancing into the
light from time to time cannot hurt, however.

What can I do to keep from getting bored during my phototherapy sessions?

You may engage in any stationary activity such as reading, writing, watching television, knitting, doing a
crossword puzzle, eating, working at a computer, or
chatting on the phone during your treatments. If you
mount your light box on a floor stand, you can exercise
on a treadmill or ski machine during your phototherapy sessions. Do not walk away or turn away from
your light box in the middle of a session. Also, do not
nap or close your eyes for more than a few seconds.

What does the light visor look like?

The light visor is shaped like a sun visor you might
wear while playing tennis. It weighs about eight
ounces and is made primarily of plastic.

How is the visor used?

Powered by rechargeable batteries or an AC wall
outlet, the visor is worn on the head over the eyes. It
produces up to 3,000 lux—far less than a light box.
However, the light source is only a couple of inches
from the eyes. In general, you would need to wear a
visor forty-five minutes to an hour to the receive the
same light dose you would get sitting in front of a
10,000-lux light box for fifteen to twenty minutes.

Can I walk around while wearing a light visor?

Yes, in fact mobility is a major selling point for
this device. You may cook, jog, take care of the

kids, or do almost anything except drive and shower while wearing the visor. (The visor should not get wet.) After your treatment session, it may take several minutes for your eyes to readjust to room light.

How much do light boxes and visors cost?

Light box prices range from about $250 to more than $500. Prices vary according to size, output, and sophistication of the device's technology. Accessories such as stands and carrying cases add about $30 to the cost of the unit. Shipping and handling can add another $30 or so to the tab.

Visors generally range in price from $300 to $400. One company, Bio-Brite, Inc., advertises its "deluxe visor kit"—complete with padded carrying case and a spare set of bulbs—for $369.

What is the advantage of a therapeutic desk lamp?

This product is designed to blend in with an office environment and provide up to 10,000 lux, as long as it is properly oriented toward the eyes.

Do dawn/dusk simulators alleviate SAD symptoms?

There is no definitive proof of this. Dawn/dusk simulators, also called circadian lights, do not produce bright light. The technology allows a gradual production of a normal light level in a room. It is used mainly by people who must wake up before dawn, and those who need help adjusting to new time zones or work schedules. Some people find that a gradual onset of light is more emotionally comfortable and less distressing than waking up in the middle of a dark winter morning.

Kirk Renaud, chief executive officer of Bio-Brite, a Bethesda, Maryland, company that sells dawn simulators as well as visors and light boxes, calls the simulator a "legitimate tool" to help people wake up in the morning. "How can you use your (light) visor if you can't wake up?" he quips in explaining how the simulator can be a useful adjunct to phototherapy.

Presumably to help its jet-lagged guests wake up in new time zones, Hilton Hotels recently installed circadian lights in twenty-five "Sleep-Tight rooms" in five U.S. cities, *Newsweek* reported in July 1997.

Can I rent a phototherapy device?

A growing number of doctors, researchers, hospitals, mental-health centers, mood disorder units, and sleep disorder clinics are purchasing light boxes and visors and making them available for loan or rent to patients. Some light box companies also rent the devices. One company charges $100 for a two-week rental and deducts the rental fee from the purchase price if you decide to buy it.

What are the advantages to renting?

It can save you money in the long run. It is difficult to predict who will benefit from light therapy, and some people balk at spending several hundred dollars on a device that could turn out to be useless. Also, renting or borrowing the equipment first can help you decide between a light box and visor.

Is free light therapy available?

Yes, if you are willing to volunteer for a SAD clinical research study. If accepted into a study, you will probably have to submit to a series of blood, saliva, and urine tests as well as physical and psychological exams and monitoring. You may also need to keep a diary of your mood and energy level. In exchange, you would receive free treatment, and perhaps a small stipend.

Several SAD research projects are ongoing in the United States and Canada, and recruitment of volunteers typically begins in late summer and early fall. Your doctor may be able to refer you to a clinical research center. For $7, the Society for Light Treatment and Biological Rhythms will send you a "SAD Information Packet," which includes a list of research programs. The society's address and phone number appear in Appendix D.

Are light boxes and visors approved by the FDA?

No. Phototherapy devices have not been evaluated by the federal Food and Drug Administration and thus may not be marketed in the United States as medical devices, according to Sharon Snider, FDA spokeswoman. Before approving devices for medical use, the FDA "has to see scientific proof that they are safe and that they work," Ms. Snider says. If a device is not approved by the FDA, she says, "the consumer has no assurance that it's safe or effective."

In the absence of FDA approval, it is illegal for light box companies to make direct medical claims as to their products' effectiveness. Nonetheless, company catalogs and Web sites teem with carefully worded information about SAD, jet lag, insomnia, all of which may be helped by light therapy. In addition to technical information about their products, many companies also offer data from published research papers demonstrating the effectiveness of phototherapy.

"The FDA looks at all sources of promotion and advertising across the board, and when we find things illegally marketed as medical devices, we send a warning letter," Ms. Snider says. "The letters usually do the trick, although these claims seem to pop up again." According to Snider, the FDA has sent about a half dozen warning letters to light box companies since 1992.

Ms. Snider says she isn't allowed to discuss whether any company has applied for FDA approval of a light box or visor. She did say, however, that the FDA has never denied such a request.

If light therapy devices are not FDA approved, why are they being recommended by so many doctors?

Based on the scientific literature, the American Psychiatric Association, the U.S. Public Health Service Agency for Health Care Policy, and the Society for Light Treatment and Biological Rhythms have deemed phototherapy a legitimate treatment for SAD and have published guidelines for its use. The fact that the FDA has not investigated phototherapy devices may simply mean that none of the light box companies has bothered to seek FDA approval. Companies typically must invest millions of dollars in research in an effort to get their product federally labeled as a drug or medical device. Light box companies are somewhat of a cottage industry in the United States and may lack the financial resources to go through a lengthy approval process—with the risk of being turned down.

How can I tell whether a light device is safe and effective?

In the absence of governmental oversight, consumers must use common sense when shopping for a phototherapy unit. Ask your doctor to recommend a device that follows clinical specifications set forth in the medical literature. Avoid devices that use incandescent lightbulbs, which can harm the eyes. Patronize a company that has been in business for several years, offers a trial period, money-back guarantee, and repair policy. If a company urges consumers to use the device only in consultation with a health-care professional, it implies integrity and awareness that people might have undiagnosed conditions that could be aggravated by light therapy. Avoid any company that guarantees success.

Advises Mr. Renaud of Bio-Brite: "Any responsible participant in this industry will not make outright medical claims." Another mark of quality, Renaud says, is membership in the Circadian Lighting Association, an industry trade group that independently tests phototherapy devices. Those tests include the use of calibrated light meters to make sure the devices are producing appropriate lux levels at various distances, Renaud says. At this writing, members of the Circadian Lighting Association included Apollo Light Systems; Bio-Brite; Enviro-Med, Inc.; Lighting Resources; Northern Light Technologies; and the SunBox Co.; among others. Addresses and phone numbers appear in Appendix A, and many companies also maintain Web sites. Here are some questions to ask before buying one of their products:

- Does your device meet the therapeutic and safety standards established through clinical tests?
- Has the device's output been calibrated for an appropriate therapeutic effect?
- Has the unit been evaluated for compatibility of components? (Some light box companies contract large architectural light manufacturers to make their products.)
- Has the unit been evaluated for visual comfort?
- Does heat buildup stay within safety limits when the unit is turned to maximum intensity?
- Does the light box or visor filter out all or almost all ultraviolet radiation?
- Does your company manufacture the devices it sells? (If not, how does it ensure that its products meet therapeutic standards?)
- Can I obtain a refund if the device doesn't work?

Your doctor, therapist, or mood disorder clinic may be able to help you decide which product to buy. By the same token, by wary of any clinician who offers to sell you a device directly. He or she may be padding the price to make a profit.

Where can I buy a light box?

Light boxes and visors may be purchased directly through manufacturers. With the exception of dawn/ dusk simulators, light devices are not generally sold through retail outlets for several reasons. For one thing, light boxes are not perceived as strong selling items, explains Jed Immel-Brown, president of Lighting Resources, a light box company in Columbus, Ohio. Since light devices are not FDA approved, retailers may wish to avoid the potential liability of selling them, Immel-Brown says. Possibly for the same reasons, major light fixture manufacturers don't tend to market phototherapy units, he adds.

Can I create a therapeutically lit indoor environment without the aid of a light box?

No. Even if you put 100-watt bulbs in every lamp and fixture in your house, you couldn't come close to creating the intensity of light needed to treat winter depression effectively.

Do light therapy devices duplicate natural light?

Not entirely. Light boxes and visors deliver a full-spectrum white fluorescent light designed to mimic the intensity of sunlight available on a summer morning. Unlike the sun, properly designed therapeutic lights produce no harmful ultraviolet (UV) rays. UV radiation, which is also present in many tanning salons, can cause sunburn, skin cancer, and eye damage. Fortunately, UV radiation is not needed to effectively treat SAD symptoms.

Which is better, the light box or the visor?

If used as directed, both can be equally effective, although the duration of treatment with the visor generally needs to be longer than with the light box, research shows. Which device you choose depends on your lifestyle and personal preference. Joe, the New Jersey retiree, bought a big light box in 1995 but didn't like it. "Unless it's at the right angle, it

doesn't work. And you have to be positioned just
perfectly and sit still, which very few people can do,"
he asserts. "Then my psychiatrist recommended the
visor, which allows me to walk around, as well as
read and watch TV. For me, the visor is far more effective than the big box, which I now have and don't
know what to do with."

According to the Circadian Lighting Association,
the light box is generally preferred by people "who
like to sit quietly in the same place each day, while
the visor is usually favored by people who want to be
mobile during their daily lighting routine. Because
it fits easily into a suitcase, the visor tends to be hand-
ier for frequent fliers. The main disadvantages to the
visor are that it requires longer phototherapy sessions, and the batteries must be recharged periodi-
cally. Also, some people are uncomfortable wearing
the visor.

Light boxes seem simple enough. Why not build my own?

Unless you are a licensed electrician with access to
a calibrated light meter and scientific expertise in
phototherapy, you would be flirting with danger. At
least two fires have been sparked by homemade light
boxes, according to Neal Owens, president and co-
founder of The SunBox Company. Owens says he
also knows of six people who suffered irreversible
eye damage "from self-treatment with homemade
devices." It may be that those devices did not filter
out all the ultraviolet light, or they exceeded the
safety threshold of about 10,000 lux, Mr. Owens
speculates. "There have even been health-care professionals who told patients to go out and buy a cou-

ple of spotlights or halogen lights, mount them on a block of wood, and look directly into them," Mr. Owens reports. "That is a recipe for eye damage."

How many people are using phototherapy devices?

In 1997, it was estimated that light boxes and visors were being used by more than 12,000 people, mostly SAD sufferers, in the United States, according to Mr. Owens.

Do health insurance plans cover light boxes and visors?

That depends on your plan. Many insurers are skeptical because phototherapy devices are somewhat new, not FDA-sanctioned, not prescription items, and not highly regulated. Also, SAD itself is a relatively new diagnostic category. Generally, if your health plan covers psychiatric treatment for SAD, there's a better-than-average chance that it will also cover claims for phototherapy devices, as well as follow-up care. However, reimbursement for your light device may not be automatic.

In Appendix B, there is a model letter that your health-care provider can fill in and send to your insurer along with your claim for reimbursement. This letter may increase your odds for coverage, but it does not guarantee it. If your claim is denied, consider filing an appeal, or arguing your case to a customer service representative. You may find someone who is educable with regard to the problems encountered by SAD patients and the proven value of phototherapy.

What would happen if I wore sunglasses during light therapy?

The effectiveness of your therapy session would be reduced.

Can I obtain a therapeutic dose of light in a tanning salon?

No. Tanning salons generally require customers to wear eye protection, which would reduce any therapeutic value from the get-go. If you exposed your eyes to tanning light, you could damage your eyes because the amount of light produced in tanning salons is probably more than you need to treat your SAD symptoms. Moreover, tanning beds and booths do not filter out harmful UV radiation.

Is phototherapy likely to get rid of all my symptoms?

That varies from person to person. Some patients enjoy a full remission from depression as a result of light therapy. Others achieve only a partial remission.

If phototherapy provides only partial relief, can I also take an antidepressant?

Absolutely. Phototherapy and antidepressants can work synergistically. In fact, many people are able to reduce their phototherapy session if they are also taking an antidepressant. It may take some trial and error before the ideal combination is found for you. There is one caution: Some antidepressants (as well as lithium) can cause photosensitivity, making the retina more sensitive to light. It is prudent to check with an ophthalmologist or psychopharmacologist—

a specialist in psychiatric medications—before beginning combination therapy. (Many psychiatrists are also psychopharmacologists.)

Should I discontinue light therapy as soon as my symptoms disappear?

No. By doing so, you run a high risk of recurrence. Most patients need to continue daily phototherapy until spring.

What would happen if I skip a few phototherapy sessions?

You would probably see a return of your SAD symptoms in three or four days, perhaps sooner. Some people can skip phototherapy one to three days without ill effect.

Should I use my light device all year?

No. Once spring returns, the longer days of natural light will normalize your mood as it does every spring. You probably won't need your light box again until the next fall.

Will my mood improve faster if I use my light box more than recommended?

No. The notion that "if a little is good, then a lot is better" doesn't hold true with light therapy. Overexposing yourself to light in the morning can make you restless and anxious. Too much light therapy in the evening can produce insomnia. It is best to stick to the regimen your therapist recommends. If you are dissatisfied with the results, say so. As mentioned previously, phototherapy's effectiveness can often be enhanced by adjusting the light's intensity, changing the time of day you use your light box, or shortening or lengthening your phototherapy sessions.

Is light therapy ever used in conjunction with psychotherapy?

Yes. These two forms of therapy can be complementary. As light therapy lifts depressive symptoms, you will be able to see your problems more clearly and objectively. That in turn will help you progress more rapidly in psychotherapy. Conversely, weekly or bi-weekly psychotherapy sessions enable the therapist to closely monitor the effectiveness and modify your treatment protocol, if necessary. Additionally, your therapist can help you identify early SAD symptoms so you'll know when to begin light therapy next year. Sometimes, getting diagnosed with SAD offers an opportunity to deal with other problems in your life.

Will I need to wean myself off light therapy as spring approaches?

There is nothing in the medical literature indicating that weaning off phototherapy is necessary. As the days grow longer, depressive symptoms tend to remit spontaneously. If you have been successfully treating your depression with phototherapy all winter, you can probably cut off treatment around mid-April or early May without risking a rebound of symptoms.

What are the contraindications to phototherapy?

When appropriately administered, light therapy can be safely used by virtually anyone, studies suggest. There is no known association between light therapy and eye disease, such as glaucoma, cataracts, or retinal diseases. Because the technology is still new, however, investigators generally exclude people with these conditions from research studies as a safety precaution. If you have macular degeneration, retinitis pigmentosa, diabetic retinopathy, or another eye condition, it is important to get clearance from your ophthalmologist before commencing phototherapy.

Can taking a winter vacation close to the equator replace phototherapy?

Temporarily. If you are going to Florida, Hawaii, the Caribbean, or any tropical region for a week or two, leave your light box or visor behind. Same goes for South Africa and other parts of the southern hemisphere where seasons are reversed. Unfortunately, the anti-SAD benefits of your sun-drenched holiday won't last long after you come home. To prevent depression from setting in again, be sure to resume your phototherapy routine as soon as possible after your vacation.

I live in New England. Will moving to Florida or Arizona get rid of my SAD for good?

There are no guarantees, of course, but for many SAD sufferers, relocating to a sunnier part of the country is curative. People usually cite the lower cost of living, warm climate, or relaxing lifestyle as fueling their desire to live in the southern United States. Subconsciously, they may also know that the additional sunshine will improve their mood.

I always feel blue when it's cloudy or raining for a few days in the spring and summer. Would a light box be helpful under these circumstances?

Yes. People like you who are particularly sensitive to light changes probably would benefit from phototherapy on overcast days. Use the same protocol that worked for you throughout the winter. Soon as the sun breaks through, you can safely halt treatment.

Chapter Six
PSYCHOTHERAPY

What is psychotherapy?

Psychotherapy, also known as talk therapy or talking treatment, uses psychological techniques to help alleviate depression or other mental disorders. In therapy, you describe your symptoms, problems, and experiences with a therapist who, in turn, provides insightful feedback. The discussion may focus on your past or present thoughts, behaviors, emotions, and relationships. Your therapist's role is not to solve your problems, but to help you figure out your own solutions. Your therapist does this by asking carefully crafted questions and making observations designed to give you a better understanding of yourself, your relationships, and your problems. In addition, psychotherapy can help you identify negative behavioral and thinking patterns and transform them into more positive ones. The goal of psychotherapy is not only to help treat your depression, but also to improve your overall outlook on life.

Is psychotherapy helpful in the treatment of seasonal affective disorder?

It can be, especially if your cyclical depressions dredge up unresolved conflicts, relationship difficulties, or other problems. For some SAD patients, getting diagnosed is a conduit to psychotherapy. In many cases, a course of psychotherapy can help SAD patients cope with depression in winter and create a more balanced, productive life in every season.

Is psychotherapy the same as counseling?

Not really, although supportive psychotherapy (described later in this chapter) comes close. Instead of helping you find your own path, counseling usually presents you with a path, or a choice of paths. The emphasis is on the here and now. The counselor does at least as much or more talking than you to provide hope, guidelines, and information. Counseling can be effective for people who aren't psychologically minded, who don't want psychotherapy, or who have a specific problem they need to resolve.

A form of counseling known as psycho-education is almost always offered to SAD patients as soon as they are diagnosed. Basically, the therapist educates the patient about seasonal mood disorders and explains how the various treatments work. In addition, patients may be given statistics on SAD, which help them to realize that they are far from alone in their seasonal suffering.

Psycho-education can often be completed in one or two forty-five-minute sessions. Armed with a fuller understanding of SAD, patients are more likely to comply with treatment recommendations.

What distinguishes psychotherapy from counseling?

While counseling places more responsibility on the counselor, psychotherapy places a greater responsibility on you to recognize negative or destructive patterns in your life and to pursue ways of breaking those patterns. As you discuss past and current feelings and experiences, the therapist serves as a catalyst for your self-discovery.

In psychotherapy, your relationship with your therapist is deeper and more complex than it would be in a counseling situation. This relationship is established through two key psychological mechanisms: 1) a therapeutic alliance, and 2) transference. A therapeutic alliance refers to the *conscious* working relationship that you and your therapist develop in order to meet common goals, such as alleviating your depressive symptoms and teaching you how to cope when those symptoms return. In transference, your *unconscious* thoughts, feelings, and reactions toward significant others are transferred or projected onto your therapist. An effective transference—be it negative or positive—is both cathartic and therapeutic. Transference and a therapeutic alliance may also form through counseling, but to a lesser degree.

How does transference work?

Say you had a condescending, overly critical mother. Unbeknownst to you and your therapist, your mother has been a major source of your low self-esteem and depression, which flower during SAD episodes. In therapy, the anxiety, fear, and ambivalence you feel toward your mother flow out unconsciously and are transferred onto the therapist. Without realizing it, you are relating to the therapist in the same way you relate to your mother. This gives your therapist strong hints of how you think, feel, and react outside of your therapy sessions. Your therapist can then hold up a psychological mirror so you can see your words and behaviors more clearly, and perhaps more objectively.

Ultimately, you may talk to your therapist as though he or she *were* your mother. The therapist could, in a sense, become the kind of mother you always wished you had: someone who supports your endeavors, someone with whom you can share thoughts and feelings without fear of belittlement.

Here is another example: An associate lawyer keeps getting bumped from law firm to law firm and never makes partner, even though he is very smart and good at his job. Growing up, the lawyer had a rocky relationship with his father and learned to buck authority figures. As an adult, this attitude persisted, manifesting in the lawyer doing something or other to sabotage his relationship with each of his bosses. In therapy, the lawyer's attitude toward authority gets replicated: He is late for appointments, or he grows hostile and nasty toward his therapist (another authority figure). Once the lawyer has transferred his feelings toward his father onto his therapist, the therapist can say, "Do you see what's happening here?" This precipitates a breakthrough in therapy. For the first time, the lawyer becomes conscious of his disdain of authority and realizes why he keeps getting fired.

Transference, even if it is not utilized so directly, is vital to your therapist's ability to help you.

How many types of psychotherapy are there?

At least seven forms of psychotherapy are in use today. Two—cognitive-behavioral therapy and interpersonal therapy—were developed with a specific focus on depression, although other forms of psychotherapy also are used to help depressed patients.

In brief, the psychotherapeutic disciplines are:

- *Classical psychoanalysis.* Developed by Sigmund Freud (1856–1939), classical psychoanalysis is the oldest and least interactive discipline. The patient lies on a couch and, through "stream of consciousness," speaks whatever thoughts come to mind. The therapist is out of sight, sitting behind the patient and doing very little talking. A great deal of time is spent looking at all the powerful components of the patient's childhood and how they combined to form his or her personality. Therapy sessions are held up to five times a week for many years. Because classical psychoanalysis is designed to restructure the patient's personality, and because it take so long, Freud's method is rarely used to treat depression. Classical psychoanalysis is one of the options for those who want a lengthy, detailed investigation of their personality structure and want to make significant modifications.

- *Traditional psychodynamic psychotherapy.* Like classical psychoanalysis, this modality uses early childhood experiences, the unconscious, and transference, but does so with the patient and therapist sitting face-to-face. It is thus more interactive than Freudian psychoanalysis. Traditional (versus brief) psychodynamic psychotherapy looks at personality patterns that may be related to the onset and exacerbation of depression. Severely depressed people who combine this form of psychotherapy with antidepressant medication tend to do quite well.

- *Supportive psychotherapy.* Like counseling, supportive psychotherapy focuses on the here and now. The therapist provides more guidance, advice, and direction than is available through any other psychotherapeutic treatment. The duration of therapy ranges from several weeks to several months, depending on the complexity of the patient's depression. Many psychiatrists, psychologists, and social workers provide supportive psychotherapy as well as other forms of psychotherapy. Supportive psychotherapy clearly has a place in the treatment of depression, although it has not been rigorously studied.

• *Cognitive-behavioral psychotherapy.* Originated by Aaron T. Beck at the University of Pennsylvania in the 1970s, cognitive-behavioral psychotherapy turned Freudian psychology upside down. Freud had said that how we feel influences how we think; Beck postulated that how we think influences how we feel. Inappropriately negative thoughts, or "cognitive distortions," can lead to depression, according to Beck's research. So the focus in cognitive-behavioral therapy is to explore your unconscious, your automatic thought patterns, and how those patterns affect your view of yourself, your environment, and your future. One example of distorted thinking is calling yourself a "stupid idiot" because you lost your favorite pen. Beyond thinking you are stupid, you also assume you'll always lose your pen and anything else that has importance and worth. In cognitive-therapy parlance, this kind of distorted thinking is known as an "all-or-none conclusion."

The behavioral prong of Beck's method entails the use of homework assignments. Your therapist may ask you to keep a log of how you are thinking or reacting under certain circumstances. Later, you can rewrite your cognitive distortions into more positive, more realistic language. For instance, "I'm a stupid idiot for losing my favorite pen" might be transformed into, "I misplaced my favorite pen, but I'm sure it will turn up eventually."

Another log entry might describe a miserable time you had at a dinner party because Tom walked by without saying hello. You instantly assumed that Tom doesn't like you, and therefore nobody at the party likes you. In therapy, you acknowledge the possibility that Tom simply didn't see you as he made his way to the hors d'oeuvre table. You also realize that Tom's opinion has nothing to do with how others might feel toward you.

The duration of cognitive therapy is variable, lasting from several months to more than a year of weekly sessions, depending on the patient's needs.

• *Interpersonal psychotherapy (IPT)*. IPT focuses on the conflicts, distortions, and difficulties that people have in their relationships with others. In session, the therapist and patient try to understand how unhealthy relationships, or unhealthy reactions within those relationships, may lead to or intensify depression. The goals of IPT are to reduce symptoms of depression, enhance your self-esteem, and improve your social functioning. IPT was developed by Gerald Klerman and Myrna Weissman for the treatment of depression over the last twenty years, and more recently by John Markowitz at Cornell University. To date, at least two research studies have shown that IPT significantly reduces symptoms in severely depressed patients.

• *Brief psychotherapy*. There are a number of different models of brief psychotherapy, but the one that has been studied most is brief psycho-dynamic therapy, which is a more abbreviated style of traditional psychodynamic psychotherapy described above. The hallmark of all the brief therapies is specific goals. For example, the goal of brief psychodynamic psychotherapy is to specifically understand how the past has led to depression. Brief cognitive psychotherapy might concentrate on one type of cognitive distortion and how it is feeding your depression. In brief therapy, the therapist plays a more active role, providing frequent interpretations and insights. Your past experiences, unconscious, and transference are all used, but in a more condensed form. "Brief" is a relative term. The treatment may last anywhere from a few weeks to a year. In general, short-term therapies lasting six weeks or less are insufficient for people with major depressive disorder. People with milder depressions can probably benefit from a course of treatment lasting sixteen weeks or less.

• *Pluralistic psychotherapy.* This approach folds certain aspects of various psychotherapeutic techniques into one treatment. For example, your therapist might focus on your relationships, your cognitive distortions, and your childhood at different points during your treatment. A pluralistic approach can become sloppy if the therapist is not well versed in all the modalities. Pluralistic psychotherapy can be effective if a depressed patient doesn't respond to a single form of talk therapy.

If I say, "I hate myself," what might my therapist's response be? Wouldn't it differ according to the psychotherapeutic method she is using?

Yes. In psychoanalysis, your therapist would probably ask, "When have you felt that way before?" and "How does it make you feel now?"

In cognitive-behavioral therapy, the response could

be, "What are you thinking that makes you conclude that you hate yourself?"

In interpersonal therapy, your therapist might say, "What goes on in your relationships with other people that makes you hate yourself?"

Wouldn't it be better for my therapist to simply point out that I have many good qualities and that I shouldn't hate myself?

Naturally, a primary goal in psychotherapy is for depressed patients to recognize and embrace their positive, admirable qualities. However, it is rarely helpful for a therapist to simply point out those qualities. Doing this could make the therapist appear too wise, which risks further diminishing a depressed patient's self-image. The impact of treatment is far more powerful and long-lasting when your therapist helps you do your own psychological work in order to discover and acknowledge your positive attributes.

Which form of psychotherapy works best in SAD?

Any of the aforementioned modalities can be adapted to help those with seasonal depression, although cognitive-behavioral therapy is probably the most widely used.

What happens during a typical cognitive-behavioral therapy session?

The cognitive aspect of therapy focuses on the flood of negative thoughts that occur during your depressive season. You will be encouraged to frequently remind yourself that all your negative thoughts and emotions are not representative of the rest of your life. Just because you have SAD does not mean you are incompetent. You still have the capacity to be content and satisfied. You are simply experiencing a biological condition that creates many of these negative thoughts and self-criticisms.

The behavioral aspect of therapy will focus on all the things you can do to combat seasonal depression. Let's say it's October, and you begin to feel overwhelmed and overworked, and you think your life is spinning out of control. If the weather is reasonably good, your therapist will urge you to take a walk outside to do a few chores that force you out of the house. Or expose yourself to bright light on your coffee break or lunch hour, even if it's just sitting in an atrium or room with a skylight. At the same time, you can employ some of your cognitive therapy techniques, such as reminding yourself that your problem is not with you, but the time of year. Another behavioral technique is to identify all those commitments and activities that are optional. During a SAD episode, you can expect that much of your energy will be sapped. Getting an idea of what you can safely delete from your schedule makes sense until you can get on top of your depression through phototherapy or some other treatment.

How does a therapist determine whether psychotherapy is indicated?

There are no hard-and-fast rules. Some people are eager to gain a deeper understanding of themselves, their behaviors, and their relationships through psychotherapy. Others are more reticent. Still others respond so well to light therapy or antidepressants that psychotherapy becomes redundant.

How many psychotherapy sessions are needed, on average?

Many SAD patients need just one or two psycho-educational sessions to learn about their disorder and to get started on light therapy. If a longer thera-peutic relationship is desired, you might have ses-sions with your therapist once a week over a period of six weeks to six months, or longer, depending on the complexity of your problem.

Can SAD be effectively treated by psychotherapy alone?

Probably not. While psychotherapy can help you sort out psychological issues brought to a head by SAD, it is unlikely to normalize the physiological changes that are causing your seasonal mood disor-der. Probably the best treatment for those who desire psychotherapy is to combine it with phototherapy or antidepressant treatment.

How much does a psychotherapy session cost?

Fees vary, with psychiatrists generally charging the most, up to $300 for an initial consultation and $125 to $250 for a forty-five- to fifty-minute therapy ses-sion. (Fees in major metropolitan areas are generally higher than in the Midwest and rural areas.) Psycholo-gists charge slightly less, followed by clinical social workers. Some offices and community mental-health centers offer sliding-scale fees to qualifying patients.

Is group therapy helpful in the treatment of SAD?

Group therapy has efficacy, although this modality has not been rigorously studied. Professionally led group therapy can be beneficial when coupled with individual psychotherapy, medication, or light therapy. Peer-led support groups and twelve-step programs can also be useful adjuncts to psychotherapy.

How long does a psychotherapy session last?

In almost all cases, a psychotherapy session runs forty-five to fifty minutes. With the exception of classical psychoanalysis, sessions normally take place every one to three weeks. Some therapists prefer to hold sessions twice a week, especially if your functioning is severely impaired or there are concerns about your safety.

How many sessions will I have to go through before I start feeling better?

That depends on several factors, including your therapist's skill, how severe or complex your depression is, and whether you are taking an antidepressant or using light therapy. Many patients feel some relief after the first session because they are finally doing something about their problem. If your depression is alleviated or made less severe by other treatments, psychotherapy may progress more rapidly. In some cases, psychotherapy makes you feel worse before it makes you feel better.

What if I develop a crush on my therapist?

You should bring it up in therapy and talk it through. Therapists are trained to deal with these situations and to conceal and manage any discomfort they might feel. Therapists are further trained not to take advantage of patients' vulnerability. If your therapist returns your affections, either verbally or physically, it is a serious breach of professional ethics. By becoming romantically involved with a patient, the therapist risks losing his or her license to practice—and you risk emotional devastation.

If talking with your therapist about your attraction fails to water down your feelings, it makes sense to consult another therapist. The consulting therapist should be able to tell you whether to change or to continue therapy and wait for your romantic feelings to dissipate.

The development of strong emotional reactions, including sexual ones, toward your therapist can occur regardless of your therapist's age, appearance, or gender. Some patients want to become their therapist's "best friend." Less common is falling in love with your therapist, a phenomenon known as erotic transference. In reality, erotic transference is a form of resistance—building an unconscious (not willful) emotional barrier to the therapeutic process. By the same token, if you never develop any strong feelings toward your therapist, it could mean that an effective therapeutic relationship is not developing.

Is it ever appropriate to hug my therapist?

Most often not. The psychotherapeutic environment is a safe haven, and a hug can have very different meanings at different times, depending on how you are feeling toward your therapist at the moment. If you are having an erotic transference, you might misconstrue a hug as a come-on. If you are having a negative transference, a hug might make you feel uncomfortable. Of course, therapists try to maintain a sense of humanity. They may shake your hand hello, give you an encouraging pat on the upper back while saying goodbye, or hand you a tissue if you are crying. It may be appropriate to give each other a hug at the close of the therapeutic relationship. Aside from these scenarios, it is inappropriate and unprofessional for a therapist to hug, kiss, or otherwise touch a patient. The therapist's goal should be to help you feel huggable to the rest of the world.

Will I look forward to my therapy sessions, or will I dread them?

That will depend largely on how you feel about the notion of psychotherapy. In the beginning, some people breathe an enormous sigh of relief as they walk into their therapist's office; others are filled with trepidation or anxiety. As the course of therapy evolves, the nature of your relationship with the therapist, as well as the nature of your transference, will dictate whether you look forward to your sessions. Be aware that your feelings about therapy and your therapist will probably change from session to session. This is normal. Some days, you may not be in the mood for having your psyche probed. Other days, you'll look forward to venting pent-up frustrations in the safe environment of your therapist's office. If you *always* look forward to therapy—or *always* dread it—there is probably something wrong.

I cannot fathom spilling out my problems to a therapist whose life is probably so much better than mine. How can I overcome these feelings of powerlessness and jealousy?

It may help to focus on your areas of expertise. Your therapist is an expert in understanding human behavior; and you have a lot to share about yourself. You are embarking on a therapeutic journey with a person whose life's work is devoted to helping people.

Resenting or envying your therapist because his or her life is allegedly better than yours can make the journey take longer. Just because your therapist seems mentally healthy now, he or she may have had depression or another emotional problem in the past. We are all human and all potentially vulnerable.

I am a very private person. What if I wish to keep certain feelings or experiences to myself?

It probably won't affect your treatment outcome. Simply state up-front that there are certain issues you do not want to discuss in therapy. Your therapist should be willing to respect your boundaries. Lying to hide a secret or to test your therapist's perceptions is probably not in your best interest. Therapists are not mind readers, and they are not always as perceptive as people assume they are. If you want to deceive or trick your therapist, you can.

Remember that psychotherapy is a collaboration. It is perfectly appropriate to hold certain secrets close to your heart. Your therapist does not need to know everything about your life in order to help you. Nonetheless, at the end of an early session, many therapists routinely ask, "Is there anything you want to tell me that might be embarrassing or upsetting that you should probably tell me anyway?" Asking such a question doesn't necessarily mean you will disclose information, but it does give you permission to do so. By asking this question, your therapist is sending you a signal that he or she has the strength and nonjudgmental attitude to tolerate whatever you might say. The embarrassing slice of your life you get off your chest may very well fit into a pattern the therapist is seeing in you. But if your deep, dark secret is that you beat up Sammy Smith in the third grade, it may have nothing to do with your current mood disorder.

In a sense, you and your therapist are painting a canvas together. You need not fill in each and every cloud or ray of sunshine, but both of you must be able to recognize what's in the picture.

Is it good to let myself cry during therapy?

Yes. But if you want to cry for forty-five minutes straight, you can do it much less expensively at home.

How am I supposed to feel after a therapy session?

You will most likely experience a wide range of feelings after your sessions. Depending on your mood and what happened during therapy, you may feel less depressed, more depressed, enlightened, provoked, annoyed, energized, or emotionally drained. Psychotherapy is not designed to be an easy process. You will be rolling up your emotional sleeves and working very, very hard to understand yourself better and to conquer your depression. Even if a session is particularly difficult, you should still walk away feeling that the encounter had value. At the end of each session, you should feel that the therapeutic alliance continues to exist between you and your therapist, and that your connection with your therapist is a positive one. These feelings are central to a healthy psychotherapeutic experience.

Do health insurance plans normally cover psychotherapy for SAD?

Coverage depends on the type of plan you have. If your plan covers psychiatric treatment, it may cover only a limited number of mental-health visits per year; lifetime caps on mental-health treatment are not unusual. As a result, many patients pay for all or part of their treatment out-of-pocket.

I've heard that therapists recommend many more sessions than are needed just so they can make more money. How can I prevent this from happening to me?

A certain percentage of mental-health practitioners take psychotherapy beyond its reasonable limits. This may happen because:

1. they are not trained well enough to know how and when to end therapy;
2. they are greedy;
3. they have made a very strong attachment to their patient and cannot let go; or
4. the clinical situation is very complicated.

To prevent your sessions from continuing endlessly, you should always be willing to say, "Where are we in therapy?" or "Is it time to stop?" Some people with SAD feel comfortable ending psychotherapy in spring when their symptoms go into remission. Others need to continue in order to fully work out all their problems. If psychotherapy is effective, you probably won't need it again if SAD returns because you will already have learned coping skills.

Regardless of the patient's diagnosis, all forms of

psychotherapy attempt to have a beginning, middle, and end. If your therapist cannot give you an indication of where you are and how far you have to go, it could be a bad sign. At this point, you may wish to consult with another therapist to get an outside evaluation of your progress.

Sometimes patients develop a resistance during the course of psychotherapy; they'll want to drop out of treatment prematurely because a therapist they previously liked now seems offensive. If this happens to you, try to evaluate your treatment based on all your sessions, not on an isolated disconcerting remark or single session. Figuring out the appropriate time to end therapy is much more art than science.

Is family therapy ever indicated for SAD?

Family therapy can be quite useful in helping your spouse, parents, or children understand why you seem to turn into a different person in the fall and winter. The key is to help your loved ones realize that your mood and behavioral changes are driven by forces beyond anyone's control. The therapist can help assuage any irrational guilt or blame your family members might harbor. Specifically, your loved ones can learn how to anticipate your mood changes, how to better cope with them, and how to help you stick to your phototherapy schedule, for example.

Can I expect a smooth course of recovery, or will there be setbacks before I get healthy again?

The latter is more likely to be true. Human emotion, behavior, and experience cannot be plotted on a perfectly smooth curve. The same goes for psychotherapy, where many of your feelings, behaviors, and experiences get replicated. Occasional setbacks are part of the process.

It may help to think of depression as a frozen pond, and recovery from depression as the melting process. Ponds don't melt uniformly; they crack in places, refreeze in others, and turn into slush. But inevitably, when springtime comes, all the ice is gone.

Can psychotherapy backfire?

Yes. Usually it happens because the psychotherapist is either incompetent or uses an inappropriate form of psychotherapy, or the patient is overtly or covertly self-destructive.

Take, for example, a man in a severe SAD episode, and he has an enormous amount of suppressed anger. He also tends to rationalize—he concocts elaborate but untruthful explanations to hide the genuine motivations behind his actions, thoughts, and feelings. Each time he rationalizes in session, his therapist points out what he is doing and suggests that his rationalizations are preventing him from getting to the heart of his depression. The patient, who has a tremendous fear of losing control, grows visibly uncomfortable and anxious each time the therapist addresses his deep-seated self-defense mechanism. Finally, in a fit of anger and frustration, the patient quits therapy and feels worse than he did before he began.

An astute therapist should know when someone's self-protective mechanisms are best left alone. An antidepressant or phototherapy coupled with a less probing, more intellectual approach, such as cognitive-behavioral psychotherapy, probably would have been more effective in this particular patient's case.

How can I be sure my therapist will maintain my confidentiality?

It is unlikely that a therapist will have a position of respect in any community if he or she does not maintain patient confidentiality. The issue of confidentiality is taught and ingrained from day one of any therapeutic training program, be it psychiatry, psychology, or social work. If confidentiality is not maintained, people and colleagues know that, and the therapist won't get referrals.

The only time a therapist must, by law, breach confidentiality is when a patient is imminently suicidal, homicidal, or is sexually abusing a minor. Here, the therapist has the legal, ethical, and moral responsibility to intervene. The therapist might give the patient a choice of a going to the hospital voluntarily, having the therapist petition the court for an involuntary commitment, or setting up a system whereby a significant other keeps tabs on the patient. There are cases where therapists themselves called a rescue squad to take a suicidal patient to the hospital.

How do therapists keep track of all their patients?

New therapists and therapists in training typically take copious notes of psychotherapy sessions; they may even tape record them, with the patient's permission. But after a while, therapists learn to remember what goes on in a session in the same way they would recall an hour-long conversation with a friend. To do their jobs well, therapists must be active listeners; they need to concentrate on what you are expressing in order to give you meaningful feedback. A few key words jotted into your chart after each session is generally enough to jog an experienced therapist's memory—even if you are one of a dozen depressed patients the therapist saw that week. Memorizing what goes on in therapy becomes as automatic as driving a car.

Chapter Seven

ANTIDEPRESSANTS

What is an antidepressant?

An antidepressant is a drug that can remove depressive symptoms by changing the function and structure of brain tissue. Despite what you may have heard or assumed, prescription antidepressants are not "happy pills," and they do not make you "high." In fact, mentally healthy people who take an antidepressant feel no difference in their mood. In people who are clinically depressed, antidepressants are designed to lift the mood directly and indirectly by blocking the negative aspects of depression. Feelings of low self-esteem and worthlessness, lack of interest, lethargy, carbohydrate cravings, hypersomnia, and virtually all the symptoms of depression evaporate. In addition, the medication helps restore the patient's energy level and powers of concentration.

An herb with possible antidepressant effects is St. John's wort. Although St. John's wort shows promise in the treatment of mild to moderate depressions, its safety and effectiveness have not been thoroughly tested in the United States. A detailed discussion of St. John's wort appears later in this chapter, where you will also find information on the potential antidepressant effects of acupuncture, exercise, and meditation.

How were antidepressant drugs discovered?

As with many scientific breakthroughs, the first antidepressant was discovered serendipitously. In 1952, iproniazid, a derivative of an antibiotic used to manage tubercular infections, was given to patients with tuberculosis (TB). The drug did not work particularly well against TB, but doctors noticed a compelling side effect: The TB patients who took iproniazid enjoyed a prolonged elevation in their mood. Imipramine, the second drug found to produce antidepressant effects, was introduced in 1957. Subsequent antidepressants were developed based on chemical structures of the known antidepressants.

How many antidepressants are there?

More than two dozen antidepressants are approved for use in the United States, and more are always under development. The most frequently prescribed antidepressants fall into one of six drug classes, or families: monoamine oxidase inhibitors (MAOI), the oldest class; tricyclic antidepressants (TCA); selective serotonin reuptake inhibitor (SSRI), the newest class; tetracyclic antidepressants; "novel or heterocyclic" antidepressants; and stimulants.

Following is a list of the major antidepressants in each category. Drugs are identified by their generic names followed by their brand names:

Monoamine Oxidase Inhibitors
phenelzine (Nardil)
tranylcypromine (Parnate)
selegiline (Eldepryl)

Tricyclic Antidepressants
amitriptyline (Elavil, Endep, Enovil)
clomipramine (Anafranil)
desipramine (Norpramin, Pertofrane)
doxepin (Adapin, Sinequan)
imipramine (Tofranil)
nortriptyline (Aventyl, Pamelor)
protripyline (Vivactil)
trimipramine (Surmontil)

Selective Serotonin Reuptake Inhibitors
fluoxetine (Prozac)
fluvoxamine (Luvox)
paroxetine (Paxil)
sertraline (Zoloft)

Tetracyclic Antidepressants
amoxapine (Asendin)
maprotiline (Ludiomil)

Novel or Heterocyclic Antidepressants
bupropion (Wellbutrin)
mirtazapine (Remeron)
nefazodone (Serzone)
trazodone (Desyrel)
venlafaxine (Effexor)

Stimulants/Amphetamines
methylphenidate (Ritalin)
dextroamphetamine (Dexedrine, Adderall)
pemoline (Cylert)

There is yet another family of drugs, the mood sta-
bilizers, that are occasionally prescribed for SAD or
classical depression. These include lithium (Cibalith-S,
Lithane, and others), valproic acid (Depakote), carba-

mazepine (Tegretol, Epitol), lamotrigine (Lamictal), and gabapentin (Neurontin).

Which antidepressants are best for people with seasonal affective disorder?

Prozac, Paxil, and the other SSRIs are the drugs of choice for people with SAD, primarily because of convenience, not superiority. Compared with the older antidepressants, SSRIs tend to have fewer side effects, need to be taken just once a day in most cases, and are considered safer in an overdose situation. All these factors lead to better patient compliance with medication schedules. SSRIs also tend to have a stimulating effect when people first start taking these drugs. This can be helpful to SAD patients, who tend to oversleep. Over time, SSRIs can become more sedating. If that happens, you may take your antidepressant at night instead of in the morning. Research has shown SSRIs to be effective and safe for short-term seasonal use (four to six months a year).

Are other types of antidepressants used for SAD?

Yes. Any antidepressant may be used to combat seasonal affective disorder. If SSRIs do not help, your doctor may prescribe Wellbutrin, which also has a stimulating effect, as does Vivactil. Unfortunately, Vivactil may also produce more annoying side effects, such as dry mouth, constipation, and blurred vision. Before trying any medication, you and your doctor should weigh all possible risks and benefits. You may be willing to put up with certain side effects if you know your depression will be effectively treated.

Why do antidepressants have such strange-sounding names?

Drugs are named and classified according to the mechanism by which they act on the brain, or to describe their molecular structure. Monoamine oxidase inhibitors, for example, inhibit monoamine oxidase—an enzyme that breaks down the neurotransmitters norepinephrine, serotonin, and dopamine. This results in more of these neurotransmitters being made available in the brain. Similarly, selective serotonin reuptake inhibitors increase the availability of serotonin to brain cells.

If you examine the molecules of the tricyclic antidepressants, you will see a three-ringed structure. Tetracyclic molecules have four rings, and heterocyclics have variable number of rings.

How do antidepressants work?

As with many medications, antidepressants' exact mechanisms of action are not fully understood. It is clear, however, that antidepressants normalize the brain's mood centers. The mood centers are a collection of brain cells, or neurons, that spread out through the brain. Neurons communicate with one another through chemicals called neurotransmitters, including serotonin and dopamine. These neurotransmitters are called first messengers because they hook up with receptors on the outside of neurons. This leads to a cascade of intercellular events known as the second messenger system, which somehow triggers DNA to make other changes in the cells that control mood.

In all forms of depression, including seasonal affective disorder, several possibilities exist:

- There may be too much or too little neurotransmitter in the brain.
- Communication between the first and second messenger systems may be incomplete.
- There may be an abnormality in the receptors on the cell surface or interior.
- One or more neurotransmitters are functioning inefficiently.

Antidepressants influence, at least indirectly, the neurotransmitters, receptors, and activity inside neurons that control mood. SSRIs, for example, selectively block the absorption, or reuptake, of serotonin in the area of the receptor. Instead of serotonin getting sucked up by the cell and pulled out of the way, an SSRI makes more serotonin available to the myriad of serotonin receptors on brain cells. So, theoretically, more serotonin attaches to more receptors, creating a greater capacity for the receptors to facilitate communication inside the mood centers.

Why are there so many different drugs for depression?

Depression is a devastating disorder that afflicts one out of every ten people in the United States and untold millions around the world. The level of human suffering and economic loss has researchers at universities, medical schools, and pharmaceutical companies working feverishly to develop better and better depression treatments with fewer adverse side effects.

In addition to the urgency of preventing suicide among depressed individuals, there is a huge economic incentive to discover more effective drugs to treat depression. Antidepressants represent a multibillion-dollar-a-year industry. Patients normally take an antidepressant daily for a minimum of six months; some people with nonseasonal depressions remain on medication for the rest of their lives. With the majority of depressed people currently untreated, the potential to relieve suffering—and to increase profits—through awareness campaigns is astronomical.

Why has Prozac gotten so much more media attention than the other antidepressants?

Discovered in Europe in 1974, Prozac was the first SSRI to reach the United States. Since its FDA approval in the late 1980s, Prozac has earned a reputation of being a very, very effective antidepressant that works on a great many serotonin receptors in the brain. Its impact on brain chemistry is so far-reaching that it became the first drug used for three psychiatric diagnoses: depression, obsessive-compulsive disorder, and panic disorder. It is no surprise, then, that Prozac initially was seen as the magic bullet that Americans always seem to be searching for.

Unfortunately, the early excitement over Prozac included a lot of misinformation, and a huge public controversy over the drug ensued. In the early 1990s, the book *Listening to Prozac* by Peter D. Kramer asserted that Prozac not only treated depression but also modified personality and intelligence. Soon afterward, *Talking Back to Prozac* by Peter R. and Ginger Ross Breggin emphasized Prozac's potential downsides, including sexual dysfunction and anxiety. Then came *Beyond Prozac* by Michael J. Norden, which focused on natural depression antidotes and prevention. These books fueled the raging debate over the risks and benefits of Prozac and other anti-depressants. All the controversy made Prozac a celebrity drug in the 1990s, just as the powerful anti-anxiety drug, Xanax, grabbed headlines in the 1980s, and Valium became a media darling in the 1970s. Next year, some other psychotropic drug will likely get all the attention.

In reality, Prozac is probably no better or worse than the other SSRIs. SSRIs are safer for the heart than some other classes of antidepressants, but SSRIs can cause headaches, tremors, agitation, nervousness, and insomnia, as well as sexual dysfunction in both men and women. SSRIs do not, however, trigger panic attacks when taken as directed. And they do not alter your personality, although they may help to reduce shyness. People who did not know you before your disorder set in may see you as a "new person." In truth, you are getting back to your normal self. By taking Prozac or any antidepressant, you are modifying an underlying, diagnosable psychiatric disorder—not reshaping your soul.

Will I have to take any blood tests before starting antidepressant treatment?

Yes. If your blood has not yet been screened for other possible causes of depression, your doctor will probably order the same battery of blood tests listed in Chapter Two. These include the "chem screen," complete blood count (CBC), and thyroid profile. You may also have an electrocardiogram (EKG). In addition, there should be a urinalysis to check for normal kidney function because many antidepressant metabolites (byproducts of the drug after it is broken down by the body) are excreted through the kidneys.

Will I need blood tests while taking an antidepressant?

It depends on which drug you are taking. Some anti-depressants, such as Pamelor, have a "therapeutic window"; the drug won't work if you are taking too little or too much. A blood test is the best way to de-termine if you are taking an appropriate dose. Any-one on a tricyclic antidepressant should undergo periodic blood tests to make sure the correct amount of medicine is in the blood since too much can be-come toxic.

Researchers have recently identified certain mark-ers in the blood that signal a problem in long-term Prozac users. It seems that some people who take Prozac, or other SSRIs, for an extended period of time (months for some, years for others) get tired. This places them at risk of falling asleep at the wheel. SSRI-induced fatigue is associated with the buildup of a certain metabolite in the blood. If this happens, the patient is often taken off medication for several weeks to allow the metabolite to wash out of the blood before resuming treatment. Patients, particu-larly Prozac users, who follow this new strategy usu-ally get their energy back. Depression usually remains in remission because SSRIs have a long-lasting effect in the brain.

Patients taking other antidepressants potentially would benefit from periodic blood monitoring, but tests do not yet exist for all of them. Ultimately, doctors hope to have blood tests for every anti-depressant on the market.

If I start taking an antidepressant in September or October, can I prevent the onset of SAD?

The research into treating depression early with anti-depressants has produced very mixed results: Some data suggest that if you use medication before symptoms become serious, you can prevent SAD from becoming full-blown. Other data show that medication doesn't really work until the symptoms are strong and consistent, indicating a full neuro-chemical change has occurred in the brain.

Will I need to take my antidepressant all year or just in fall and winter?

If your depression is biologically linked to the timing and intensity of light exposure, you should be able to wean yourself off medication in the spring with little risk of recurrence—until, perhaps, the following fall or winter. Since there is no evidence to suggest that once you've experienced SAD, it will always recur, taking an antidepressant all year may expose you to adverse side effects needlessly while also wasting money. Indeed, taking an antidepressant four to six months this year may actually protect you from a recurrence next year, even if you have suffered from untreated SAD five years in a row. It is also possible that a good, vigorous treatment—perhaps involving both an antidepressant and light therapy—can break the SAD cycle forever.

Will an antidepressant curb my carbohydrate cravings?

Indirectly. There is no evidence to suggest that anti-depressants suppress the appetite. However, once

the antidepressant has normalized the level of serotonin and other chemicals in the brain, the body
may instinctively reduce its cravings for carbohydrates. It is believed that overeating starches and
sugars helps the brain, in some complex way, make
more serotonin.

Should I take appetite suppressants to reduce my SAD-induced cravings?

No. As a rule, attempting to treat any symptom of
depression in isolation is not recommended because
it ignores the core problem. It is much safer to treat
the depression directly because that should alleviate
most or all of your symptoms. Also, none of the prescription appetite suppressants have been shown to
provide a consistent and reliable antidepressant effect. And some have raised serious health concerns.

How long must I take an antidepressant before I begin to feel better?

The time it takes for an antidepressant to work
ranges from one to six weeks, with an average of two
to four weeks. However, up to 35 percent of people
who take an antidepressant experience an immediate
positive placebo effect because they expect the medication to work. Positive side effects also may emerge
soon after starting drug therapy. For example, a
stimulating antidepressant may begin to reduce your
need for sleep after the first or second dose. Sleeping
seven hours instead of eleven itself may impart an
antidepressant effect.

Why don't antidepressants alleviate depressive symptoms faster?

Antidepressants work on a long, slow, complex cascade of events involved in intercellular communication in the brain. Also, antidepressants are administered in small but increasing dosages until a therapeutic level of the drug is reached in the bloodstream. The slow-acting nature of all antidepressants, and the urgency at which severely depressed patients need relief, has researchers looking for new antidepressants that act more quickly.

What does it feel like to be on an antidepressant?

In time, you will probably feel like your old self again, which may give you a dramatic sense of relief. The increased sense of well-being you feel may stem from the disappearance of your depressive symptoms, as well as from the drug itself. Or, you may not realize the benefits of your treatment until much later, when you examine your mood in retrospect.

What percentage of SAD patients who take an antidepressant get better?

Statistically, 65 to 85 percent of depressed people who take an antidepressant recover. However, there are many, many psychiatrists and psychopharmacologists who believe the actual success rate exceeds 95 percent. It may take a lot of trial and error before the right drug, or combination of drugs, and the right dose of phototherapy is determined for you. But when that happens, there is an extremely good chance that SAD will go away.

Should people with severe SAD always be offered an antidepressant?

With so many relatively safe and effective SSRIs available today, SAD patients certainly have a right to antidepressants. But medication should never be forced on anyone. Many doctors urge SAD patients to try phototherapy before resorting to medication. Some people are very opposed to psychotropic drugs, anyway, and consider light therapy to be a more natural treatment modality.

How should antidepressants be taken?

While each patient's treatment plan is individualized, some generalizations can be made. As mentioned earlier, your medication will likely be started at a low dose to make sure you can tolerate it and to give your body a chance to get used to the drug's effects. If you are in good health, the dose will be increased every two or seven days, as tolerated, until it reaches its therapeutic range.

Are antidepressants ever combined with psychotherapy in the treatment of SAD?

Occasionally, when an antidepressant or light therapy alone is not sufficient to help patients work through all their problems. When used in concert, an antidepressant and psychotherapy can create a powerful one-two punch because:

1. Psychotherapy supports you emotionally until your antidepressant takes effect, or until the right antidepressant is found.
2. An antidepressant can help you regain the

emotional strength you'll need in psychotherapy to better understand yourself and the source of your depression.

3. Weekly psychotherapy has a built-in monitoring system for your medication's efficacy and side effects.

Which symptoms usually respond to antidepressants first?

There is no clear pattern, although many patients report that oversleeping is the first symptom their antidepressant begins to attack. You may also notice a very, very subtle shift in your mood initially. Within the first week or so, you may feel a little less negative, a little less hopeless and sad, or you may have a little less difficulty getting out of bed and making it through the day. As time goes on, your ability to concentrate may start to improve. You may become less irritable, and your sugar cravings may subside. There is no way to predict which symptoms will go away first, or in what order.

If you are lucky, all of your symptoms may respond to the medication and dissipate simultaneously or serially. Some antidepressant users get a little better the first week, only to find symptoms returning the next week. An erratic pattern may continue until there is a full response to the medication.

What kind of sexual problems are caused by SSRIs and the other antidepressants?

Inability to achieve orgasm, reduced or loss of sexual desire, difficulty becoming aroused during sex, inability of the penis to become or stay rigid, premature or nonexistent ejaculation, and reduced semen output all have been reported by users of antidepressant medications. SSRIs are more notorious than others for certain forms of sexual dysfunction. For example, SSRIs may slow down ejaculation and reduce sexual desire. About 60 percent of people who take an SSRI will experience these or other sexual side effects. Three antidepressants with minimal or no sexual side effects are Wellbutrin, Serzone, and Remeron.

I have no interest in sex when I am experiencing SAD. If I take an SSRI, how will I know if my reduced libido is being caused by the drug or by my depression?

Before you begin taking an antidepressant, inform your doctor of any past or current sexual problems. It may be possible to find a medication or dosage level that minimizes certain sexual side effects. At the very least, knowing your history of sexual problems will help your doctor determine later on whether a sexual symptom is connected to the medication. It is also possible that your interest in sex will return after your depression begins to lift.

Is there anything I can do to alleviate the sexual side effects of my medication?

There are a variety of ways to combat your medication's sexual side effects. For instance, your doctor may allow you to take a drug holiday by skipping your medication on Friday and Saturday if you are planning a special weekend. A different strategy is to take your antidepressant as scheduled but add another drug, such as Periactin, before you go to bed. Periactin is a serotonin antagonist; it blocks the effects of serotonin, which the antidepressant presumably is making more available to brain cells. Periactin should not be used too frequently because it will interfere with the antidepressant's beneficial effects. Also, Periactin is sedating. If you are not planning to fall asleep after making love, you may wish to try Ritalin, a stimulant, to enhance your sex drive. Because of its addiction potential, Ritalin should be used only as a last resort. Another drug your doctor may suggest is Yocon, which was originally used for male impotence. Yocon, a general sexual stimulant, does not interact with antidepressants but can make people nervous. Ginkgo biloba, a fruit-bearing tree native to China, is being investigated as a treatment for sexual side effects.

Don't be shy about discussing your sexual symptoms, side effects, or concerns with your doctor, even if the doctor neglects to ask about them. Open communication with your significant other is equally important. Unless your partner understands that your sexual symptoms are drug induced or part of your depressive illness, he or she may erroneously assume that something is wrong in your relationship.

Aside from sexual problems, are there other adverse effects associated with antidepressants?

Yes. A large number of adverse side effects have been reported by antidepressant users over the years, and the vast majority of people who take an antidepressant experience adverse effects to one degree or another. The good news is that some adverse effects subside over time. Others can be controlled by manipulating the dose or time of day you take your antidepressant, or by adding another medication to your drug regimen.

In addition to sexual dysfunction and anxiety, SSRIs may cause gastrointestinal upset (often in the form of heartburn or diarrhea), dizziness that is unrelated to blood pressure, lightheadedness, and a dull headache.

The most prominent side effects associated with the tricyclics and tetracyclics include dry mouth, constipation, difficulty urinating, postural hypotension (dizziness upon standing up abruptly owing to a drop in blood pressure), heart palpitations, blurred vision, sweating, stimulation or sedation, and weight gain, in addition to sexual difficulty.

MAOIs typically cause significant postural hypotension, difficulty with orgasm, sedation and insomnia, dry mouth, weight gain, and, more rarely, stimulation. MAOIs can also provoke a hypertensive crisis—if you eat the wrong food or take the wrong drug when you are on an MAOI, your blood pressure can rise so rapidly and dramatically that it may cause a stroke. Classic symptoms of stroke are a headache in the back of the head, along with sweats and nausea. MAOI users are now given an antidote to keep with them at all times that will take down their blood pressure, just in case.

Most of the novel or heterocyclic and tetracyclic antidepressants share similar side effects with both the tricyclics and SSRIs. The most common of these side effects are stimulation or sedation, stomach upset, and lightheadedness. Overall, people on MAOIs or tricyclics feel more "drugged" than people who take SSRIs or novel or heterocyclic antidepressants.

A list of possible side effects will accompany your prescription. Provided by your pharmacy, these lists are comprehensive and may include side effects that are frightening but extraordinarily rare. Discuss any concerns you might have with your doctor.

What I can do to lessen some of the nonsexual side affects of my antidepressant?

Here are some things you can try:

• To relieve constipation, drink eight glasses of water a day, increase your intake of live acidophilus cultures (found in yogurt and acidophilus milk), and consume foods high in soluble fiber. If you use a Metamucil-type laxative, do not take it with your medication because the fiber may not allow as much absorption of the drug.

• To relieve dry mouth, drink lots of water, suck sugar-free hard candy, or eat frozen green grapes. Dry mouth may also respond to one of the over-the-counter preparations, such as Saliva Substitute. If all else fails, your doctor may recommend Salogen, a prescription drug designed to increase saliva flow.

• If your antidepressant makes you dizzy when you stand up quickly, simply stand up more slowly. You may also want to increase your salt intake if your blood pressure is low in general.

• The dull headaches associated with SSRIs are treatable with any of the nonprescription analgesics.

• You can compensate for blurred vision by holding reading material at a slightly greater distance from your face than usual. Be extra careful when driving a car. If you will be taking your antidepressant for a long period of time, wearing glasses or changing your prescription glasses may help. Blurred vision, far more common with the tricyclics than any other class of antidepressants, tends to scare patients because they think there is something wrong with their eyes. Fortunately, this effect is transient. Check with your doctor first if you are considering getting a new eyeglass prescription.

Knowing what to expect before you begin drug treatment will help you plan your coping strategies. Your doctor should explain which side effects to anticipate. For example, knowing in advance about postural hypotension could mean the difference between falling as you rise from a chair and preventing injury because you deliberately stood up slowly.

Can antidepressants cause cancer?

There are no hard or consistent data showing that any of the antidepressants cause or exacerbate cancer. In fact, antidepressants are frequently prescribed to cancer patients to help improve their mood.

Has anyone ever died from taking an antidepressant?

Yes. Death by antidepressants is exceedingly rare, but it can happen in several ways. You could suffer a fatal allergic reaction called anaphylactic shock. In almost fifty years of antidepressant use worldwide, only a handful of these cases have been reported. If your medication is improperly prescribed and inadequately monitored, you can have a sudden cardiac arrest. Also, a willful overdose can result in death. Tricyclics's effect on the cardiovascular system makes them particularly dangerous. If taken all at once, a one- or two-week supply can produce serious, potentially fatal cardiac complications. In fact, tricyclic antidepressants are now the leading cause of death by drug overdose in the United States. It is a cruel irony that medications so effective in combating suicidal depressions have such potential lethality. Fortunately, the newer antidepressants (for example, the SSRIs) are safer in an overdose situation.

Will I experience side effects before the drug begins to work on my depression?

That depends. Some people feel worse before they begin to feel better. This is one reason doctors normally prescribe a low dose and work up to a therapeutic dose over the course of several weeks. Try not to let the adverse effects discourage you. Let the fact that your body is being affected by the medication give you hope that you will soon enjoy a positive response. If possible, take your first dose at a time of day when your doctor is easily accessible, in case you have a bad reaction.

Do adverse side effects worsen or lessen over time?

Again, there is no predictable pattern to the severity or duration of antidepressant side effects. Some will go away on their own, others will not.

Why would anyone choose an antidepressant over light therapy, which seems so much more benign?

There are several possible reasons:

- You have a blood relative with SAD who responded well to an antidepressant;
- You would rather swallow a pill once a day

instead of spending thirty minutes or more a
day wearing a light visor or sitting in front of a
light box;

• You are skeptical of light therapy;

• Your insurance covers the cost of antidepressants
but not light devices;

• Your seasonal depression is complicated by other
psychiatric problems, such as dysthymia or
obsessive-compulsive disorder, which may also
be alleviated by certain antidepressants; or

• Your seasonal depression occurs in summer
rather than winter; summer depressions do not
ordinarily respond to light therapy.

**Given all the adverse side effects, why would anyone
want to take an antidepressant in the first place?**

The consequences of not treating depression effectively are potentially more serious than any adverse
side effects. As a result, many patients perceive side
effects as mere annoyances, not deterrents to treatment. Nevertheless, you and your physician should
carefully analyze the risk/benefit ratio before you decide whether to take an antidepressant. In some
cases, the risk of adverse effects is not worth the potential gain. So, if your SAD symptoms tend to be
mild, and you drive a truck or work with power
tools for a living, it may not be prudent to take an
antidepressant that can potentially make you tired. If
you are a teacher with SAD, and light therapy hasn't
helped, the potential benefits of taking an antidepressant probably outweigh the risk since your depressive season encompasses a significant chunk of the
school year. If you are debilitated by your depression

every winter, side effects seem like no big deal if the antidepressant can help you reclaim your life.

Can antidepressants affect my dreams?

Yes. Virtually all antidepressants have the capacity to alter sleep architecture, including REM (rapid-eye movement) sleep—the stage of regular dreaming—and stage 4 sleep—the time when frightening dreams and nightmares can occur. Patients, especially those taking SSRIs, often report more vivid dreams.

After going off your medication, your REM-stage dreams may temporarily increase in intensity and frequency. This phenomenon is known as "REM rebound."

Are allergies to antidepressants common?

No. Less than five percent of patients will develop a rash, usually within twenty-one days of starting medication. Severe or life-threatening allergic reactions to antidepressants occur in a very tiny percentage of the population—far less than one percent.

If I develop a rash from taking one kind of antidepressant, should I avoid other antidepressants in the same class?

Not necessarily. Rashes are caused by a drug's chemical structure, not its function. If you are allergic to Paxil, for example, you may still be able to use another SSRI such as Prozac or Zoloft, which have different chemical structures.

Can antidepressants affect my fertility or ability to carry a pregnancy to term?

There is no consistent or reliable research assessing the fertility rate among antidepressant users, although antidepressants can theoretically affect the menstrual cycle. There are no significant data suggesting antidepressants appreciably increase the risk of miscarriage.

Is it safe to take an antidepressant during pregnancy?

The little research that has been done to answer this question has yielded somewhat mixed results. One study out of the University of California-San Diego looked at several hundred women who had taken Prozac during pregnancy. No increase in the risk of miscarriage or major birth defects was found. Taking Prozac in the third trimester did, however, increase the newborn's risk for low birth weight, breathing difficulties, and other minor problems, according to the study. A more recent study by Toronto researchers found that prenatal exposure to Prozac or a tricyclic antidepressant made no difference in a young child's IQ, behavior, temperament, or language skills. Although these two small studies—published in the *New England Journal of Medicine* in October 1996 and January 1997, respectively—offer reason for optimism, their findings have yet to be replicated by larger studies. Also, there are no controlled studies examining the long-term effects of prenatal exposure to antidepressants, although preliminary data look reassuring.

Unless her depression is life-threatening, a pregnant

woman with SAD should probably try phototherapy or talk therapy first. If she is still depressed, she should avoid antidepressants during the first trimester, if possible. After that, she should weigh the unknown risks to her baby against the known risks that depressive symptoms place on a pregnancy. For example, a severely depressed woman who doesn't take her vitamins or get proper prenatal care is putting her baby's health at risk. Depression that continues after the baby is born can interfere with mother-infant bonding.

Will I harm my baby if I take an antidepressant while breast-feeding?

All antidepressants pass into breast milk, but it is unknown whether this hurts the baby or whether the baby will experience withdrawal symptoms after weaning. Most psychiatrists recommend against breast-feeding while on an antidepressant. Infant formula may be less ideal than breast milk, but a depressed mother cannot nurture her baby as well as she could if her depression were adequately treated.

What are the chances that the first antidepressant I try will work?

Research has shown that between 50 and 60 percent of patients respond to initial antidepressant treatment. Of those who don't, the majority get better after switching medications.

What will happen if I have to switch antidepressants because the first one didn't work?

That depends on the medications involved. If you are switching from one of the MAOIs (Nardil or Parnate), you must wait at least two weeks before starting treatment with another antidepressant. If you are switching *to* an MAOI from Prozac, you must wait five weeks (two weeks if you were taking one of the other SSRIs). Otherwise, too much serotonin can build up in your system. This can cause a life-threatening stroke, or a condition known as serotonin syndrome. Symptoms of serotonin syndrome include restlessness, tremors, muscle spasms, and confusion. In Chapter Nine, you will find a variety of ways to cope with your depression until your new medication begins to work.

Just because your first antidepressant isn't doing much to alleviate your depressive symptoms, that doesn't necessarily mean you have to switch medications. Sometimes, taking a second antidepressant will kick-start your medication into action. Your doctor may try adding a small amount of tricyclic to an SSRI regimen, for example. Or you might try augmenting your treatment with an entirely different drug, such as lithium, Cytomel (the thyroid hormone T3), BuSpar (a nonaddictive anti-anxiety drug), Parlodel (an anti-Parkinson's drug), Tindal (used to treat a variety of emotional disorders), or Visken (a beta-blocker normally used to treat high blood pressure or migraines). Stimulants, such as Ritalin, are also sometimes used to augment treatment.

You should not consider augmentation until your antidepressant has had sufficient time to work on its own—at least four weeks. If you do augment, you may or may not need to take the additional medication throughout your full course of treatment.

What is the typical dosage schedule for antidepressants?

SSRIs and most of the other antidepressants are usually taken once a day. Effexor and Serzone should be taken twice a day because their half-life (the amount of time it takes your body to metabolize half the amount of drug in your system) is relatively short. This dose schedule could very well change as newer versions of these drugs emerge. For example, Wellbutrin, historically taken three times a day, now comes in a sustained-release preparation and may be taken twice daily.

Patients are usually started with a small dose and gradually work up to a therapeutic dose. In the case of Prozac, the therapeutic dose is twenty milligrams for most depression patients.

If you combine an antidepressant with phototherapy, you may be able to get away with a slightly lower medication dose, shorter phototherapy sessions, or both. For example, if you are on Prozac, you may need only fifteen minutes with your light box at 10,000 lux instead of twenty minutes. Many patients who use this dual treatment approach like the idea that their antidepressant serves as a backup should they miss a day of phototherapy. Work with your doctor to determine the combination treatment that is best for you.

Should antidepressants be taken on a full stomach?

Not necessarily. However, if your antidepressant produces gastrointestinal distress when taken on an empty stomach, you may take it with food to prevent that side effect.

What are the contraindications for antidepressants?

In SAD patients who also have undiagnosed or untreated bipolar disorder, antidepressants can shift depression to mania. If you have high blood pressure, probably the only antidepressant you'll need to be more careful with is Effexor, which may raise blood pressure. If you have low blood pressure, you should avoid tricyclics and MAOIs, both of which can decrease blood pressure. You should also be wary of the tricyclics if you have hyperthyroidism, heart problems (such as mitral valve prolapse), or any systemic disease that increases the heart rate. People with irritable bowel syndrome may have to avoid SSRIs, which can cause diarrhea. Certain antidepressants and dose levels are potentially harmful to patients with heart, liver, or kidney disease.

Are there any medications I should avoid while taking an antidepressant?

It is dangerous to take certain antihistamines, such as Seldane and Hismanal, while on an SSRI. Anticholinergic and sympathomimetic medications (used in certain allergy and cold remedies, as well as in anesthesia, some gastrointestinal medications, and certain ophthalmologic drugs) may aggravate the side effects of some of the tricyclic antidepressants. Do not worry, however, if you need emergency surgery while on an antidepressant. Chances are there will be no significant adverse drug interaction. Surgeons and anesthesiologists are well-trained to monitor patients for drug interactions.

How often will I need to see my doctor while I am taking an antidepressant?

Usually, patients need one or two appointments to establish a diagnosis before getting a prescription. If you are to have psychotherapy, your practitioner can monitor your response to the medication during your regular sessions. Otherwise, you will probably be asked to come in or call after two to four weeks of antidepressant treatment to report how you are feeling and whether you are having any adverse side effects. Naturally, if you have a severe or unexpected reaction, you should notify your doctor immediately. Once you are stabilized on medication—which can take anywhere from two weeks to three months— your doctor will probably want to see you about once a month to monitor your blood pressure and side effects and to observe and discuss your clinical response. If you are to discontinue your antidepressant in the spring, your doctor will tell you when to start reducing your dose so you can be weaned off medication.

How much do antidepressants cost?

Depending on where you live, which pharmacy you use, and sometimes your dosage, antidepressants average about $1.60 to $2 a day. That translates to $48 to $60 a month, or $292 to $365 for a six-month course of treatment. Some drug companies vary prices according to the amount of medicine in each pill; others charge the same regardless of dose.

My health plan doesn't cover prescription drugs. Is there any way of cutting my costs?

Yes. Ask your psychiatrist for free samples left by drug company representatives. If paying for your medication is a hardship, your doctor may be able to give you up to several months' worth of samples. Another way to save money is through the drug companies themselves. Most drug companies have mechanisms to provide a limited amount of antidepressants free to patients who could not otherwise afford them. Ask your doctor how you can take advantage of these programs.

Using generics also can lower your costs. Many antidepressants, including all the tricyclics, come in these less expensive versions. Unfortunately, generic antidepressants have a wide range of variability, so their potency and bioavailability are less predictable than those of the name brands.

Are there any foods I should avoid while taking an SSRI?

Unlike the MAOIs (Nardil, Parnate), SSRIs have no dietary restrictions. MAOIs should not be combined with sauerkraut or marmite (a green vegetable jelly from Britain). Other foods and beverages to be avoided by MAOI users include beer, red wine, aged or smoked cheese, brewer's yeast, liver, pâté, soy sauce, fava beans; herring, sausage, and other smoked or picked meat, fish, and poultry; and many types of Chinese food. All these substances are high in the amino acid, tyramine. If you are taking an MAOI, you are blocking an enzyme that usually breaks down tyramine. By eating the aforementioned foods, a tyramine buildup can occur, dangerously raising blood pressure.

Can I safely drink alcohol or smoke marijuana while on an antidepressant?

Probably not. While imbibing during antidepressant therapy is not necessarily dangerous, research suggests it can undermine the effectiveness of your medication, especially during the first few months of treatment. Also, alcohol may aggravate your symptoms or slow your recovery rate. For these reasons, doctors advise patients to abstain, or at least to keep alcohol consumption to a bare minimum, while on antidepressant medication.

Marijuana is also probably best avoided. Marijuana's active ingredient, THC, is a hallucinogen and probably acts on the same neurotransmitters being manipulated by antidepressants. Also, THC is fat soluble, so it lingers in the brain for a long time. For similar reasons, cocaine and other illicit drugs should also be avoided.

Can antidepressants make a person commit suicide?

Not directly. Ironically, the greatest risk of suicide occurs during that window of time when people begin to regain energy but are still depressed because their antidepressant has not fully normalized thought patterns and judgment. Once their energy returns, some depressed patients find the willpower to kill themselves.

Several years ago, a controversial study found that Prozac increased the user's suicide risk. When the research was systemically reviewed, however, the data were found to be flawed; there was no evidence that

Prozac led to or caused suicide. Yet, there is a very, very rare phenomenon where patients report feeling suicidal when taking an antidepressant when they did not feel suicidal before. Experts are not sure what to make of these reports. It may be a pharmacological effect, or a psychodynamic effect. Perhaps it stems from an inappropriate sense of failure or shame for having to resort to medication.

Both patient and mental-health professional must be vigilant regarding the patient's feelings about suicide. These feelings can often be dispelled through good psychotherapy combined with a strong support network of family and friends.

Will my antidepressant's effectiveness wear off over time?

A small minority of patients will build up a tolerance of their antidepressant and require a larger dose. In a few cases, antidepressants stop working entirely. The reasons for these phenomena are only beginning to be probed.

Can children with SAD safely take antidepressants?

Yes, but their antidepressant should be prescribed by a competent child psychiatrist who has training in psychopharmacology.

Are antidepressants addictive or habit forming?

Antidepressants may produce some mild, non-dangerous symptoms when they are discontinued. People can also become psychologically dependent on their antidepressant. Interestingly, patients who protest going on an antidepressant in the beginning are often the most skittish about coming off them later on. They feel so good that they are afraid their depression will return.

Will I have withdrawal symptoms when I stop taking my antidepressant?

Probably not—if you are weaned off your medication slowly. If you stop taking your antidepressant cold turkey, your withdrawal symptoms will vary according to which drug you were on. Tricyclic antidepressant withdrawal symptoms may include nausea, vomiting, and drooling. Abrupt cessation of SSRIs can produce a transient "head rush," or sense of electricity in the head. The other antidepressants also can cause some minor discomfort, including headaches and malaise, when you stop taking them. Fortunately, withdrawal symptoms are not dangerous.

Coming off antidepressants gradually has other possible advantages. It may reduce the risk for a recurring SAD episode.

What would happen if I stopped taking my medication prematurely?

Depressive symptoms could rebound. Research indicates that if you stop taking your antidepressant before four months, there is an 80 percent chance that your depression will come back.

ST. JOHN'S WORT

What is St. John's wort?

St. John's wort (*Hypericum perforatum*) is a yellow, flowering plant that people have been ingesting for an estimated 2,000 years. Over the last fifteen years,

St. John's wort ("wort" is Old English for "plant" or "herb") has been used as a remedy for mild to moderate depression in Europe with few reported side effects. In recent years, St. John's wort has garnered quite a bit of media attention in the United States for both its antidepressant properties and its potential to fight the AIDS virus.

Is St. John's wort effective against seasonal affective disorder?

This is unknown. Most of this research was conducted in Germany and published in scientific journals reportedly unfamiliar to an international audience. In 1996, the *British Medical Journal* published a meta-analysis of twenty-three of these studies involving more than 1,700 outpatients. Overall, the researchers concluded, *Hypericum* extracts were similarly effective as standard antidepressants in the treatment of mild to moderate depression. None of the studies looked at St. John's wort in the treatment of seasonal affective disorder specifically.

Also, most of the research to date doesn't include many double-blind, placebo-controlled studies, which characterize the American gold standard when investigating the efficacy and safety of new drugs. That, combined with the lack of uniform preparations of St. John's wort should, at the very least, give you pause if you are considering this remedy. For one thing, there may be other substances in *Hypericum* preparations that have unknown pharmacological properties. Also, St. John's wort may have MAOI-like side effects. In theory, the herb could raise blood pressure if taken with tyramine-rich foods listed in the previous chapter, although this has not occurred in research studies to date.

What are the adverse side effects of St. John's wort?

Digestive problems, allergic reactions, and fatigue have been reported by a small percentage of *Hypericum* users. Sensitivity to sunlight is a more common side effect, so people must use sun protection and avoid other drugs that cause photosensitivity when taking St. John's wort. This obviously could complicate matters for SAD patients, who need as much bright light exposure as possible.

Thus far, there have been no published reports of serious drug interactions involving St. John's wort, and there have been no reports of toxicity after an overdose of the herb. However, this is no guarantee that St. John's wort is safe.

Are American psychiatrists recommending St. John's wort as a treatment for depression, seasonal or otherwise?

Some are, but the majority are not. Skepticism of St. John's wort centers around these main concerns:

- There is insufficient research into the herb's long-term safety;

- Not enough is known about the herb's effectiveness;

- Virtually nothing is known about the effectiveness of St. John's wort in the treatment of SAD;

- Little is known about interactions between St.

John's wort and other herbs, drugs, foods, or
food additives; and

• There are no standards of purity for the
  Hypericum extracts, tinctures, and teas
  being sold in American health food stores
  as food supplements.

Just because a substance is "natural" doesn't always
mean it is gentle and harmless. Many powerful drugs
used against cancer and other diseases were originally
derived from plants. Safety questions and lack of large-
scale rigorous studies are the main reasons most
American psychiatrists are not recommending St.
John's wort, given the alternatives that are known to
be safe and effective for seasonal affective disorder and
other forms of depression.

That stance could very well change should large-
scale controlled studies planned in the United States
show the herb to be safe. It is entirely possible that
St. John's wort will someday be considered a legitimate weapon in the battle against depressive illnesses, including SAD. Until then, most psychiatrists
think it is too risky or cavalier to use something
that is not proven to be safe, even if it appears to be
effective.

**Despite the medical community's skepticism,
aren't depressed people trying St. John's wort
on their own?**

Yes. Many people are equally skeptical of doctors
and psychiatrists. If you want to give St. John's wort
a try, it would behoove you to at least obtain a
proper diagnosis, if you haven't done so already. For
example, there are no data showing the herb can ef-

fectively treat severe depression, and if this is your diagnosis, taking St. John's wort could be a waste of money and precious time. By delaying standard treatment in order to try an unproved remedy, you risk having your illness worsen.

If you have bipolar disorder or dysthymia that grows more severe seasonally, first discuss St. John's wort with a psychiatrist who is well versed in state-of-the-art depression treatments. Don't be persuaded by what you may have read about St. John's wort in the lay press. These accounts are not 100 percent reliable.

What might be an appropriate dosage of St. John's wort?

There are no established guidelines on dosage or length of treatment. However, the daily dosage levels most cited in the medical literature range from 0.4 to 2.7 milligrams of hypericin (*Hypericum*'s presumed active ingredient), or 300 to 1,000 milligrams of *Hypericum* extract. Most test subjects seemed to respond in four to eight weeks. You can buy St. John's wort in liquid, capsule, or dried form for tea.

How much does St. John's wort cost?

Random calls to health food stores in the New York metropolitan area revealed that it costs about $8 for sixty 250-milligram capsules, about $11 for one hundred 500-milligram capsules, and about $7 for a one-ounce bottle of extract. Directions on the extract bottle suggest taking ten to thirty drops three times a day, either directly or mixed into tea or juice.

ACUPUNCTURE

What is acupuncture?

Acupuncture is an ancient form of Chinese medicine in which specific points on the body are stimulated by hair-thin needles that are inserted and twisted, or by an electrical current. The goal is to boost the body's own healing powers by restoring the normal flow of bioelectric energy, or "qi" (pronounced "chee"). Qi flows along bodily pathways known as "meridians," with each set of points corresponding to a particular organ in the body.

Acupuncture is said to affect the structure and function of living tissue without side effects or dependency. Often combined with Chinese herbs, acupuncture is used for a wide variety of physical and mental ailments, including chronic or acute pain, digestive problems, respiratory infections, insomnia, infertility, muscle sprains, smoking cessation, drug addictions, weight control, stress reduction, as well as depression and other mood disorders.

Is there any evidence that acupuncture can effectively treat depression?

Yes. Many practitioners of this 5,000-year-old technique have reported success in treating patients with depression. In the West, researchers have recently begun to investigate acupuncture. In one sixteen-week pilot study funded by the U.S. Office of Alternative Medicine, researchers found that acupuncture treatments allayed various symptoms of mild to severe depression. The study, led by J. B. Allen, Ph.D., an assistant professor of psychology at the University of Arizona-Tucson, randomly divided thirty-eight severely depressed women into three groups: the first group received eight weeks of acupuncture treatments targeted at their depressive symptoms and administered twice a week. The second group received the same number of general acupuncture treatments that were not meant to treat depressive symptoms. The third group was put on a waiting list for eight weeks before receiving eight weeks of targeted acupuncture. None of the test subjects were imminently suicidal, although many had thoughts of suicide.

The results of the study: The first group reported a 43 percent reduction in their depressive symptoms, the second group experienced a 22 percent reduction in symptoms, and group three reported a 14 percent reduction. Of the women who received targeted acupuncture, more than half were no longer clinically depressed after eight treatments (four weeks). None had been taking antidepressant medication.

"We have submitted a grant (application) to conduct a much larger scale version of our study," Dr. Allen said, "and should those results prove similar, we will then compare acupuncture directly to existing treatments, and we will examine whether acupuncture can prevent relapse." Until the results of large-scale studies are in, depressed people should first consult with a medical specialist before running to the nearest acupuncturist.

Which points on the body were stimulated to alleviate depressive symptoms in Dr. Allen's study?

Points were stimulated in many different regions of the body—the trunk, arms, back, legs, head, and ear.

**Were there any side effects to the acupuncture
treatments?**

None that the researchers could detect. Two of the
thirty-eight test subjects dropped out, complain-
ing of discomfort with the needles. Three others
dropped out for other reasons, such as moving away
or pregnancy.

How can I find a qualified acupuncturist?

Look for someone who is a diplomate of the National
Certification Commission for Acupuncture and Orien-
tal Medicine. You can obtain a list of certified acupunc-
turists by calling the commission at (202) 232-1404. At
least thirty-five states regulate acupuncture practice.
For information on your state's laws, contact the National Acupuncture Foundation, 1718 M Street/Suite
195, Washington, D.C. 20036, or call (202) 332-5794.
This information is also available on the Internet's
World Wide Web: http://www.acupuncture.com/State
Laws/StateLaws.htm#26.
   Be sure to tell your acupuncturist about any
health problems you may have, drugs or medical devices (including cosmetic implants) you are using,
and whether you are pregnant.

How much does acupuncture cost?

One national survey revealed the average cost of
three months worth of visits was about $240. Some
health insurance plans cover acupuncture for certain
conditions. If yours is one of them, get it in writing
before beginning treatment, if finances are a concern.

Does acupuncture hurt?

If the practitioner is experienced, acupuncture needles can usually be inserted with minimal discomfort. Acupuncture needles are so thin that ten to fifteen can fit inside a single hypodermic needle.

EXERCISE

How can something as simple as exercise be an effective treatment for depression?

Aerobic exercise, when done routinely, is believed to increase the level of endorphins (the "feel-good" hormones) in the brain, albeit temporarily. In particular, slow, sustained aerobic exercise, such as swimming, riding a stationary bicycle, or walking, as well as brief, vigorous aerobic exercise, seem to have brief beneficial effects on all kinds of depression, including seasonal affective disorder. It has been shown that after exercise, levels of serotonin and norepinephrine in the brain increase, which may help alleviate depressive symptoms for several hours.

In addition to physiological benefits, exercise offers a psychological boost. Physical activity provides a way of channeling your energy and taking action. This is especially useful if you are uninterested, withdrawn, or anxious along with being depressed. Exercise releases tension and improves your overall sense of well-being and physical fitness. For people with SAD, exercising several times a week is a great way to combat winter weight gain. Organized group sports, such as volleyball and basketball, require sportsmanship and socialization, which also may improve your mood.

MEDITATION

What is meditation?

Meditation is a stress-reduction technique designed to bring your physical, mental, and emotional states into balance. There are several forms of meditation, most of which are steeped in Eastern philosophy but have been popular in the United States for more than thirty years.

One form of meditation can be done sitting or lying down, relaxing your body and quietly focusing your thoughts on your breath, a word or phrase (mantra), or a mental image. Another form of meditation, known as "mindfulness," is "being in the moment" while performing any task—paying close attention, without passing judgment, to all the sights, smells, sounds, and other sensation that you otherwise would overlook or perceive as distracting. All forms of meditation force you to carve out small blocks of time from your busy day to focus on the present moment and to let go of all other concerns. Any thoughts of the past or future that drift into your consciousness while meditating are allowed to disappear like bubbles in a glass of cola.

By meditating five to twenty minutes once or twice a day, many people feel more relaxed, more alert, and more in control of their feelings. Meditation has been shown to lower blood pressure, reduce heart and respiration rates, and increase alpha brain waves, which are associated with relaxation.

Can meditation alleviate SAD symptoms?

That depends on how severely depressed you are. Meditation is most commonly used in the West to reduce physical stress, to treat stress-related illnesses, anxiety disorders, and to control pain. It may therefore be helpful in agitated depressions and extremely helpful for people with winter blues. However, attempts at meditation can backfire on the severely depressed individual. Meditation requires concentration, and it can be difficult to concentrate during a severe SAD episode. Failed attempts at meditation threaten to exacerbate an underlying sense of hopelessness and helplessness, which can deepen the person's sense of despair. In general, the more severe your depression, the less useful meditation is likely to be.

If you want to try meditating, realize at the outset that it might not make you feel better. More important, don't get down on yourself if it doesn't work.

Do I need formal training to learn how to meditate properly?

Meditation is easy to learn, and there are many excellent books on the subject. There are also audio tapes with guided meditations. Or, you may choose to take a class in Transcendental Meditation (TM) or another meditation technique. You can learn of TM classes in your area by contacting Maharishi University of Management, 1000 North 4th Street, Fairfield, Iowa 52557, (515) 472-7000.

Remember, while meditation can be an excellent adjunct, it should not replace medicinal and psychotherapeutic treatment, especially if you are severely depressed.

Chapter Eight
PREVENTION

Can seasonal affective disorder be prevented?

In some cases, yes. As pointed out in Chapter Five, many SAD sufferers find they can prevent or minimize depression by starting daily light therapy or an antidepressant at least two weeks before symptoms can be expected to set in.

There are also alternative therapies that may help to ward off depressive symptoms or lighten their impact. These therapies will be discussed later in this chapter.

I can't remember exactly when I start feeling depressed. What are the early warning signs of seasonal depression?

As pointed out in Chapter Two, the onset of depression tends to be very insidious, so it is often difficult to become aware that depression is looming, especially if you've never kept track of your seasonal mood changes. In general though, be suspicious when symptoms are mild at first then intensify over time. Also look out for groups of symptoms, not just one.

For example, you might notice an innocuous yet consistent change in your sleep pattern. Perhaps you always went to bed at eleven P.M., fell asleep within twenty minutes, and awoke feeling refreshed when your alarm clock rang. But lately, you have been unusually tired and started taking naps or going to bed at nine. In addition, you have some mild cravings for sweets, an inexplicable crying spell or two, and you are feeling irritable or short-tempered at times. Or you can't muster enthusiasm for activities you normally enjoy, and a sense of sadness, flatness, or dullness seems to be creeping up on you.

Not everyone can tune in to subtle mood alterations. Instead, they notice behavioral changes related to their sinking mood. Difficulty getting out of bed in the morning, snapping at your spouse or children, or reading less because you cannot concentrate well are some examples. It may take several weeks for all your symptoms to build into a full-blown clinical depression. You'll know when depression hits because the symptoms will be quantitatively greater in strength and in place for at least two consecutive weeks.

Will the same symptoms that signaled previous SAD episodes herald my next episode?

In most cases, SAD is characterized by the same symptoms that had signaled your original episode. So if your most recent bout with SAD involved crying spells, agitation, oversleeping, and severe difficulty in concentration, those generally are the same markers to look for in your next episode. After your symptoms go away, your therapist may provide you with a checklist of symptoms that could possibly signal a recurrence. Your loved ones and close friends should familiarize themselves with the list so they

can guide you back into treatment should it become
necessary.

If I notice some early warning signs of a recurrence, how long should I wait before contacting my therapist?

Consult your therapist as soon as you notice some
soft, initial signs of SAD. Try to do this before those
symptoms have been in place for several weeks. It
can be very comforting, and even therapeutic, just
knowing that someone stands ready to help you.

Will spending more time outdoors in the wintertime help?

Definitely, especially if you can go outside regularly
before ten A.M. This time of the morning offers the
highest quality of wintertime sunlight. Some people
like to take a brisk morning walk. Others prefer to
sit on a park bench or sunny porch and read the
newspaper. Every minute you can spend in the sunshine can help keep depression at bay. Don't be dis-
suaded by the need to bundle up against the cold.
Remember, it's the intensity of light entering your
eyes that matters, not the amount of light reaching
your skin.

Can changing my diet help prevent SAD symptoms?

Probably not. But consuming plenty of fresh fruits,
vegetables, whole grains, and fluids may fill you up
enough to curb carbohydrate cravings. You should
also reduce or eliminate your intake of alcohol, caffeine, and sweets, and avoid all nonprescribed mood-
altering substances.

Can altering my sleep schedule make a difference?

It can. As a person with SAD, you should try to be very disciplined in terms of your sleep schedule. If you have the option to sleep late in the morning, stay up later the night before. Getting the same amount of sleep every night is one measure of good "sleep hygiene." Other measures are:

- going to sleep and waking up at roughly the same time seven days a week;
- avoiding food for two hours before bedtime;
- avoiding caffeine after noon;
- avoiding alcohol;
- avoiding naps;
- using your bed only for sleeping and making love;
- going into another room, sitting in a chair, and reading or watching television if you cannot fall asleep within thirty minutes;
- avoiding vigorous exercise at night; and
- avoiding work right before bedtime.

Can reducing stress prevent SAD?

Probably not. As emphasized throughout this book, SAD is triggered by changes in light cues. Stress may aggravate seasonal depression, but it does not trigger it.

Can I prevent SAD through psychotherapy?

Again, the answer is probably no. Psychotherapy can help you resolve problems that get intensified during your seasonal depressions. Psychotherapy can also give you tools to cope with your depression (see Chapter Nine).

Can joining a depression support group help prevent future SAD episodes?

Being with others who share your disorder is almost always beneficial. Research has shown that when people spend an inordinate amount of time by themselves, it can adversely affect their mood and their capacity to cope with adversity. The camaraderie fostered through self-help groups probably has opposite effects.

However, not everyone is comfortable in group encounters. Another tack you might try is cultivating at least one relationship in which you can discuss your depression freely. Also, the mere act of participating in a bowling league or playing basketball once a week may also be therapeutic because it forces you to be with others on a regular basis.

Can massage therapy or aroma therapy reduce SAD symptoms?

Anything you do that feels good and is safe is a positive step. Getting a massage, for example, is an act of self-respect. So is taking a long, luxurious bath to unwind after a difficult day. Being good to yourself on a regular basis raises your self-esteem, and that certainly can offer a measure of protection against some SAD symptoms.

Can certain vitamins or foods reduce my risk for SAD?

Try to maintain a diet that keeps your blood levels of vitamins and minerals within the normal range. But there is no evidence showing that any form of depression can be prevented by taking mega-doses of vitamins or minerals.

I think about suicide every time I'm in a depressive episode. Is there anything I can do to break this pattern before it is too late?

Many people, when they're depressed, experience suicidal feelings. If you did not act upon these feelings in the past, there is no suggestion you will act upon them in the future. If you feel suicidal, it is best to talk it through with someone you trust. The goal should not necessarily be to get rid of your suicidal thoughts. Rather, you should try to identify the causes behind them since suicide is not always linked to depression. Suicide can be an act of desperation, aggression, or escape, or it can be a way of punishing someone. Suicide can also be related to an unconscious fantasy of joining someone who has died.

In many cases, depression-related suicides happen during the first three depressive episodes—before the person has learned that suicidal thinking is always temporary. On the other hand, many people also become worn out by recurrent depressions and attempt suicide. Ultimately, severe depression and thoughts of suicide may go hand-in-hand. For safety reasons, suicidal thoughts during depression should not be ignored.

What are the risk factors for suicide?

A previous suicide attempt, a family history of suicide, and articulating a plan are the three most common markers for suicide. Others include being single, white, and male; advancing age; intractable pain; and the death of a spouse or loved one.

Suicidal people also may:

- make statements about hopelessness, helplessness, or worthlessness;

- be preoccupied with death;
- have an unusually large amount of guilt or shame;
- have a sense of profound professional or personal failure;
- suddenly feel happier and calmer after a long time of being depressed;
- lose interest in things they once cared about;
- visit or call people they care about;
- get their financial or legal affairs in order;
- give things away;
- be in turmoil over their sexuality.

When it comes to suicidal thoughts, mental health professionals draw an important distinction between passive and active suicidal ideation. Passive suicidal ideation would include such thoughts as, "I wouldn't mind being dead." Passive thoughts are often part of a depressive syndrome and do not usually indicate that suicide is imminent.

Active ideation would include purchasing a gun or stockpiling sleeping pills, and having a plan, such as: "On Sunday, when everyone is at the Little League game, I will kill myself." Even at this stage, however, the vast majority of suicidal people are ambivalent. It is not unusual for them to articulate their plan to a psychiatrist or someone else. This provides an opportunity to help. People who are hell-bent on suicide, however, usually don't tell a soul about their plan and carry it out successfully.

Is it ever normal for people to think about suicide?

Yes. Almost everybody has considered the notion of suicide; it appears to be a natural part of the human experience. In the depressed, the thought of suicide often provides a metaphorical door out of a room that has no other doors. In this sense, suicidal thoughts can actually be therapeutic, so long as the person does not act on those thoughts.

How common is suicide among depressed people?

Of the approximately 25,000 people who commit suicide each year in the United States, 70 percent have either depression or alcoholism, studies have shown. Events precipitating suicide among people under age thirty include separation, rejection, unemployment, and legal difficulties. For suicide victims over age thirty, illness is a more common trigger.

Chapter Nine

COPING WITH SAD

**If there are so many effective treatments for
seasonal affective disorder, why do I need to
bother with coping skills?**

There are several reasons. Under the best of circumstances, it takes several days for light therapy to
eliminate depression, and not everyone responds
completely to this intervention. Some patients need
to fiddle with the light's intensity and the length of
treatment before discovering what works best for
them. Antidepressants take up to six weeks to work.
Likewise, psychotherapy often takes several weeks to
make an impact. Anything you can do in the mean-
time to cope with your disorder on a day-to-day basis will enhance, and perhaps hasten, the effectiveness
of your treatment.

Mastering some of the coping strategies outlined
in this chapter can give you a sense of control, or em-
powerment, during a time when you feel particularly
out of control. These skills can help you preserve relationships at work, home, and in social settings. Finally, learning how to cope with a current depressive
episode may enable you to prevent or soften the
blow of any future episodes.

I suffer from wintertime blues, but I don't get clinically depressed. Can these coping skills help me, too?

Absolutely. You may find one or more of the following suggestions extremely helpful. Just ignore the items pertaining to phototherapy and medication if your condition is not severe enough to warrant those treatments.

What are the coping skills?

The following tips and strategies have helped people cope with major depression, both seasonal and nonseasonal. Some of the suggestions are self-explanatory. Those that need elaboration are discussed in more detail. The suggestions are not listed in any particular order.

One caution: Don't try to employ too many coping skills at once. Pick two or three that seem doable. If those don't help, try some others. Perhaps just one of the strategies will resonate with you. If that is the case, it may be all you need to make your life more bearable until your depression lifts. Hopefully, each of these strategies will provide a healthy counterbalance to the negative pressures of SAD.

COPING STRATEGIES

• *If you feel depressed in the morning, don't fight it.* As explained in Chapter Three, most depressed people feel their absolute worst when they wake up. One way of coping is to give yourself permission to feel horrible in the morning: Cry or wallow in self-loathing, guilt, sadness, and any other negative thoughts and emotions that depression can bring. As you let it all out, realize that your mood will most likely improve as the day wears on. When you are ready, let that realization motivate you to get of bed, shower, brush your teeth, eat breakfast, and create some structure to your day. Tomorrow morning will bring another opportunity to let your negative emotions flow unabated. As your depression begins to lift, your mornings will become much easier.

• *Try not to spend too much time alone.* Being with sympathetic friends and loved ones may help distract you from your downtrodden mood or give you a shoulder to lean on. Occasional solitude is okay, however, particularly when you feel a need to "fake it" in order to appear happy when you are with others.

• *Whenever possible, avoid people and situations that create stress or make you unhappy.*

• *Recognize times of the day when you feel better, and rearrange your schedule to take advantage of those times.* This suggestion is especially relevant in a work environment. For example, don't schedule an important meeting in the morning if this tends to be your worst time of day.

• *Divide large tasks into smaller ones.* You can increase your chances of success by tackling a series of simpler, short-term goals as a way of meeting a more complex, long-term goal. Focusing on one small task at a time also prevents you from feeling overwhelmed. Make sure your long-term goal isn't overly difficult.

• *Set priorities, and stick to them.* It may help to write a "to-do" list and rank each task in order of importance. Delete or delegate tasks when possible.

• *Lower your expectations of yourself.* You don't expect to do laundry and drive the carpool when you are sick with the flu. Why should you expect yourself to be as playful with your kids or as creative at work when you are suffering from SAD?

• *Forgive yourself for not being as productive or friendly as you normally are.*

• *Avoid taking on too much responsibility.* If someone asks you to coordinate your neighborhood block party or become den mother to your son's scout troop, give yourself permission to say no. You need not share your mental state, just explain that your plate is too full at the moment.

• *Exercise and play sports.* Feeling strong physically may help improve your psychological fitness.

• *Stick to your phototherapy schedule.* Don't become lackadaisical just because you are feeling better. Your symptoms may recur if you go too long without regular exposure to bright light.

• *Find something enjoyable to do during your phototherapy sessions.* Read a great book, or watch your favorite TV sitcom on videotape, for example.

• *Don't skip taking your antidepressant.* If you fail to take your medication as directed, your symptoms may remain the same or worsen.

• *Show up for all your psychotherapy appointments.* It is important see your therapist as scheduled in order to develop an effective therapeutic relationship and transference (see Chapter Six). If you are too ill to leave home, your therapy session can be conducted over the phone.

• *Attend sporting, cultural, religious, or social events.* These are sources of great pleasure that may help draw you out of a depressive spiral and put you in touch with like-minded people.

• *Don't make any important life decisions when you are depressed.* Skewed or poor judgment is common during a bout with SAD. If you are depressed while trying to decide whether to quit your job, for example, it will be difficult, if not impossible, to clearly consider all the implications. If you make a major decision while in the throes of any mood disorder, you risk regretting the outcome.

• *Pray.* Many people believe that prayer can have a healing influence. If you don't want to pray for yourself, pray for someone else who is in need of physical or emotional healing. Or ask someone to pray for you. If you are agnostic or atheist, try meditation.

• *Listen to or make uplifting music.* Scientific studies have shown that music stimulates the release of the neurotransmitters serotonin and norepinephrine, which can help alleviate depression and create a sense of well-being.

• *Read poetry.* But avoid poems that are too depressing.

• *Hum, sing, or whistle.*

• *Enroll in an adult-education course.* This nurtures intellectual growth and provides an opportunity to be in a group setting.

• *Volunteer.* Helping others may take your mind off your symptoms.

• *Avoid alcohol and drugs that are not prescribed by your doctor.* Alcohol and illicit drugs can make depressive symptoms worse. Certain legal drugs can cause depression as a side effect or be dangerous if mixed with an antidepressant. If you are on an antidepressant, tell your doctor if you are about to take any other prescription or over-the-counter medication.

• *Remind yourself every day that your feelings of hopelessness are caused by the time of year, and that your condition is temporary.*

• *Educate yourself about SAD.*

• *Join a support group for people with depression.*

• *Find an Internet chat room for SAD sufferers.*

• *Allow yourself one snack a day without feeling guilty.*

• *Cook a special meal and invite someone over to share it.*

• *Rediscover an old hobby, or take up a new one.*

• *Put fresh flowers in your home.*

• *Sit in a Jacuzzi, have a massage, or get a manicure.* Anything nice you can do for yourself may improve your mood.

• *Rent funny movies, read the comics, or watch Comedy Central on cable TV.* Laughter triggers the release of endorphins (natural opiates) in the brain.

• *Take a walk or bicycle ride through a park.*

• *Play with children.* Children exude unabashed joy and laughter that can be infectious. Of course, kids can also get on your nerves. Don't feel guilty should this happen. If you have a choice, it's probably best to play with children, or read to them, in short bursts.

• *Buy yourself a gift.* Treat yourself to a pretty dress, a nice piece of jewelry, a new basketball, or your favorite recording artist's new CD. Even if you don't think you deserve it, the gift can impart a sense of pride and self-worth.

• *Do something nice for someone.*

• *Go to a museum.*

• *Become involved in winter sports.* Skiing downhill or cross country, snowboarding, sledding, or riding a snowmobile are great ways to get sunlight exposure in winter. So is ice skating, as long as you use an outdoor rink.

• *Put yourself on "automatic pilot" if you can't get motivated.* Motivation often follows action.

• *If you are invited to a party, put on some makeup or your favorite sport coat and go.*

• *Don't be a perfectionist.* Perfectionism can increase your stress and worsen your depression, especially when you cannot do things perfectly.

• *Spend time with animals.* Studies have demonstrated that the simple act of petting a cat can lower blood pressure and reduce stress.

• *Rake leaves and shovel snow.* These chores may be tough physically, but they certainly force you outdoors during your depressive time of year.

• *Do a "reality check" on your automatic negative thoughts.* For example, if you think, "I'm useless. I can't do anything right," think of the last useful thing you did, such as fixing that leaky faucet, cleaning your kitchen, or teaching your six-year-old to tie his shoes.

• *Keep a diary to express your thoughts, feelings, and accomplishments.*

• *Don't demean yourself for what you haven't accomplished.*

How can I help my family cope with my seasonal depression?

The first thing you should do is let your loved ones—especially your children—know that they did not cause you to have SAD, and ultimately, they are not responsible for healing it. Next, you can seek professional help, if you haven't done so already. Bringing a therapist into the picture relieves your family of some of the responsibility and burdens of dealing with your disorder on their own. Therapy also creates a conduit through which healthy change can flow. Encourage your parents, spouse, and children to participate in any family therapy that your therapist might recommend. Family therapy provides insight into your disorder as well as concrete recommendations on how family members can help.

In general, the people you live with should maintain their current roles in the best way they can. In addition, they can let you assume the "sick role"—society's permission for someone to be ill without feeling guilty about it. While you are in the sick role, your family can relieve you of some of your responsibilities until you get better. For instance, if you normally prepare dinner, your spouse and children should take over that task.

Sometimes, the sick role is taken to unhealthy extremes: Family members continue to fawn over a depressed person who has grown excessively dependent. Or the depressed person's inappropriate aggression is tolerated, even when it hurts other members of the family. A therapist can instruct the family on how and when to draw the line, if the family cannot figure it out intuitively. Family therapy is particularly useful when one person's depression serves as a catalyst for family dysfunction. Joining a support group for families of the depressed is another valuable step your loved ones can take.

A FINAL NOTE

Each of the coping mechanisms mentioned in this chapter represents one more reason to be encouraged if you have seasonal affective disorder. As this book has repeatedly emphasized, wintertime depression is not an intractable disease with unavoidably dire consequences. Depression may cause you to feel helpless and hopeless, but you are neither—and that is the happy irony. Depression is imminently diagnosable and highly treatable.

You don't need to suffer. All you need is help.

Glossary

acupuncture: an ancient form of Chinese medicine in which specific points on the body are stimulated by hair-thin needles in order to restore the normal flow of bio-energy.

adjustment disorder with depressed mood: tearfulness, sadness, or hopelessness that is triggered by a life change.

anaphylactic shock: a potentially fatal allergic reaction.

anhedonia: loss of the capacity to experience small pleasures or to derive pleasure from daily rituals; withdrawal from pleasurable activities.

antidepressant: a drug designed to remove depressive symptoms by changing the function of the brain.

antihypertensive: any medication designed to lower high blood pressure.

atypical depression: form of depression in which there is a sad mood plus some less common symptoms, such as an ability to enjoy pleasurable situations, oversleeping, overeating, and hypersensitivity to criticism.

bioavailability: a medical term referring to the amount of active ingredient that is available to your cells after a drug has been digested.

bipolar disorder: episodes of clinical depression and periods of mania, each of which last more than a week, also known as manic depression or manic-depressive illness.

brief psychotherapy: any psychotherapeutic modality that focuses on a specific goal and is concluded after several weeks to one year of weekly sessions.

classical psychoanalysis: a form of psychotherapy developed by Sigmund Freud that focuses on the patient's childhood, personality development, and unconscious; psychotherapy sessions are usually conducted several times a week for many years.

cognitive-behavioral psychotherapy: a form of psychotherapy that helps patients identify negative thinking patterns and change them into positive ones.

cognitive distortions: inappropriately negative thoughts that may lead to depression.

complete blood count (CBC): a measurement of red and white blood cells, useful in detecting anemia, infections, allergies, and other disorders.

contraindication: a reason (usually a medical condition) for avoiding a particular drug or therapy.

counseling: a form of talking therapy in which the counselor gives a client hope, guidelines, and information aimed at solving a current problem.

dawn simulator: device that gradually turns up room light in the morning.

depression: a mental illness characterized by sadness, pessimism, hopelessness, and related feelings coupled with lack of interest or loss of pleasure lasting a minimum of two weeks.

dopamine: one of the brain chemicals believed to play a role in controlling mood.

dysthymia: a mild, chronic depression or despondency that lasts for at least two years in adults and one year in children and adolescents.

dysthymic disorder: see *dysthymia.*

efficacy: effectiveness.

erotic transference: a form of resistance that occurs when a patient falls in love with his or her therapist.

first messenger system: a process whereby neurotransmitters hook up with receptors on the outside of brain cells.

group therapy: a therapeutic setting in which a small group of people exchange information and ideas with the help of a trained facilitator, usually a psychologist, psychiatrist, or social worker.

half-life: the amount of time that half of a drug remains active in the body before being metabolized and eliminated.

heterocyclic antidepressant: an antidepressant with a variable-ringed molecular structure; e.g.: Asendin.

Hypericum perforatum: see *St. John's wort.*

hypersomnia: oversleeping.

hypertensive crisis: a sudden, dramatic rise in blood pressure, which may lead to a stroke if not treated.

hyperthyroidism: an overactive thyroid gland, often caused by an autoimmune disorder resulting in an overproduction of thyroid hormones; symptoms may mimic depression or mania.

hypomania: a mild form of mania.

insomnia: sleep difficulty.

interpersonal psychotherapy: a form of psychotherapy that focuses on conflicts, distortions, and difficulties that people have in their relationships with others.

light box: a device to deliver light that is intense enough to treat SAD symptoms.

light therapy: exposure to intense light in order to relieve symptoms of seasonal depression and certain other conditions, such as jet lag and sleep disorders; also known as phototherapy.

light visor: a device worn on the head that delivers a therapeutic dose of light to the eyes.

lux: unit of measure referring to the intensity of light at a particular location; measured by a calibrated light meter.

Lyme disease: a tick-borne illness that sometimes causes psychiatric symptoms, especially depression.

major depressive disorder: a depressed mood or loss of interest or pleasure plus other symptoms that last over a span of two or more consecutive weeks; other symptoms may include significant weight loss, difficulty concentrating, sleep disturbance, fatigue, and feelings of worthlessness.

mania: a mood disorder marked by an elevated, expansive, or irritable mood; racing thoughts; feelings of grandiosity; reduced sleep; distractibility; and poor judgment.

manic depression: see *bipolar disorder*.

meditation: a stress-reduction technique of quietly focusing on the breath, a word, or an action in order to bring the physical, mental, and emotional states into balance.

melatonin: a central nervous system hormone secreted by the pineal gland; used most commonly to prevent jet lag but may also have implications in the treatment of depression.

metabolite: a byproduct of a drug being broken down by the body.

monamine oxide inhibitors (MAOIs): a class of antidepressants that inhibit an enzyme that breaks down norepinephrine, thus making more of the neurotransmitter available in the brain.

mood center: a collection of different neurons spread throughout brain that control mood.

mood disorder: a psychiatric diagnosis that includes depression, dysthymia, bipolar disorder, and mania.

mood stabilizer: a drug that blocks both manic and depressive symptoms; i.e., lithium, valproate, or carbamazepine.

neuron: brain cell.

neurotransmitter: a chemical that facilitates communication between brain cells.

norepinephrine: one of the brain chemicals believed to play a role in controlling mood.

observing ego: the intellectual part of the psyche that can take a step back and look at life objectively even when emotions are in turmoil.

phototherapy: see *light therapy*.

placebo effect: a positive or negative effect of a drug that stems from a person's expectations rather than the drug's active ingredient.

pluralistic psychotherapy: a form of talking therapy that folds certain aspects of various psychotherapeutic techniques into one treatment.

postpartum depression: symptoms of major depression that begin within a year of giving birth and last at least two weeks.

postural hypotension: dizziness upon standing up abruptly owning to a drop in blood pressure.

psychiatrist: a medical doctor who specializes in the treatment of psychiatric illness.

psychologist: a specialist in the use of psychotherapeutic techniques to treat mental disorders.

psycho-education: a form of counseling aimed at educating patients about their disorder and its treatments.

psychomotor agitation: the visible speeding up of body movements and physical reactions, extreme nervousness.

psychomotor retardation: the visible slowing down of body movements and physical reactions.

psychopharmacologist: a psychiatrist or other medical doctor who is an expert in medications used to treat psychiatric disorders.

psychosomatic illness: any in a range of physical symptoms that can be attributed to a mental, rather than a physical, cause; also known as psychophysiologic disorder.

psychotherapist: a trained professional who uses psychological methods to help people overcome or cope with mental illness; usually a psychiatrist, psychologist, or clinical social worker; also known as "therapist."

psychotherapy: a talking treatment for mental and emotional disorders that uses psychological methods.

psychotic features: delusions, hallucinations, or other disruptions of perception that accompany depressive symptoms.

psychotropic drug: a medication that alters mood or otherwise affects the mind; antidepressants are psychotropic drugs.

receptor: an area on the surface of a brain cell where chemical messengers (neurotransmitters) attach.

REM rebound: a temporary increase in the intensity and frequency of dreams that can occur after discontinuing antidepressant medication.

REM sleep: a dream phase of sleep marked by rapid-eye movements.

resistance: a patient's unconscious building of an emotional barrier to the psychotherapeutic process.

St. John's wort: a yellow, flowering plant that is being studied in the United States as a treatment for mild to moderate depression.

seasonal affective disorder (SAD): abnormal mood and behavioral changes that recur on a seasonal basis, triggered by changes in light cues.

second messenger system: a cascade of intercellular events that trigger DNA to make changes in brain cells to control mood.

selective serotonin reuptake inhibitors (SSRIs): a class of antidepressants that increase the availability of serotonin in the brain.

serotonin: one of the brain chemicals believed to be involved in controlling mood and states of consciousness.

serotonin syndrome: restlessness, tremors, muscle spasms, and confusion that occur when there is an overload of serotonin in the brain.

sleep hygiene: sleep rules such as going to bed and waking up at the same time, and not eating or watching TV in bed.

supportive psychotherapy: a form of talking therapy that focuses on the here and now; the therapist provides more guidance, advice, and direction than is available through any other psychotherapeutic modality.

tetracyclic antidepressant: an antidepressant with a four-ringed molecular structure; e.g. Wellbutrin.

therapeutic alliance: the conscious, working relationship that develops between a psychotherapist and patient in order to meet common goals, such as alleviating depressive symptoms.

therapist: see *psychotherapist*.

traditional psychodynamic psychotherapy: a psychoanalytic modality that looks at the unconscious, early childhood development, and personality patterns related to a current mental problem.

transference: projecting onto a therapist your unconscious thoughts, feelings, and reactions, which were previously experienced with a significant other, such as a parent or sibling.

tricyclic antidepressant (TCA): an antidepressant with a three-ringed molecular structure; e.g. Tofranil.

APPENDIX A:
Selected Light Box Companies

Apollo Light Systems
352 West 1060 South
Orem, UT 84058
800-545-9667
801-226-2370

Bio-Brite, Inc.
7315 Wisconsin Avenue, Suite 1300W
Bethesda, MD 20814
800-621-5483

Enviro-Med, Inc.
1600 SE 141st Ave.
Vancouver, WA 98683
800-222-3296
360-256-6989

Lighting Resources
1421 W. 3rd Ave.
Columbus, OH 43212
800-875-8489
614-488-6841

Northern Light Technologies
8971 Henri Bourassa W
St. Laurent, Quebec H4S 1P7
Canada
800-263-0066

The Sunbox Company
19217 Orbit Dr.
Gaithersburg, MD 20879
800-548-3968
301-869-5980

APPENDIX B:

Model Letter From Doctor to Health Insurer Arguing for Reimbursement to Cover Phototherapy Device

Date_____

To Whom it May Concern:

This is to certify that _____ is a patient of mine. She/he is being treated for recurrent major depressions with a seasonal pattern. Referral to "seasonal patterns of depression" has been included in the most recent revision of the *Diagnostic and Statistical Manual of Mental Disorders (DSM-IV-R)*. Phototherapy is no longer considered experimental, but is a mainstream type of psychiatric treatment. In 1989, the American Psychiatric Association's Task Force on Treatment of Psychiatric Disorders (Vol. 3, pages 1890–1986, A.P.A. Press), recommended light therapy as treatment for the range of clinical depression diagnoses including:

Code No.:	Diagnosis
DSM-IV-R-296.3X	Major Depression, Recurrent
DSM-IV-R-296.4X	Bipolar Disorder, Manic
DSM-IV-R-296.5X	Bipolar Disorder, Depressed
DSM-IV-R-296.6X	Bipolar Disorder, Mixed
DSM-IV-R-296.7X	Bipolar Disorder, NOS
DSM-IV-R-311.00	Depressive Disorder, NOS

In order to administer phototherapy adequately, a bright
light unit is required. In _____'s case,
the use of the bright light unit should be regarded as
a medical necessity and preferable to other forms of
treatment.

These procedures conform to April 1993 US Public Health
Service Agency for the Health Care Policy and Research
guidelines for management of this disorder.

Publication #	Publication Title
AHCPR93-0551	Depress: Guideline Vol. 2
AHCPR93-0553	Depress: Patient Guide

Sincerely,

APPENDIX C:
Support Groups

The support groups listed below were provided by the Self-Help Clearinghouse, Northwest Covenant Medical Center, 25 Pocono Road, Denville, New Jersey 07834-2995. Please enclose a self-addressed, stamped envelope when writing to any of the support groups. Call the groups during normal business hours only.

National Organization for Seasonal Affective Disorder (NOSAD)
P.O. Box 40190
Washington, DC 20016
Founded 1988. Provides information and education on the causes, nature, and treatment of seasonal affective disorder. Encourages development of services to patients and families, research into causes, and treatment. Newsletter.

National Depressive and Manic Depressive Association
730 North Franklin Street, Suite 501
Chicago, IL 60610
800-826-DMDA
Founded 1986. Provides support and information for patients and families and public education on the biochemical nature of depressive illnesses. Annual conferences, chapter development guidelines, newsletter.

Depressed Anonymous
1013 Wagner Ave.
Louisville, KY 40217

Founded 1985. Twelve-step program to help depressed persons believe and hope they can feel better. Newsletter, phone support, information, referrals, pen pals, workshops, conference, seminars. Information packet ($5), group starting manual ($10.95). Newsletter.

Emotions Anonymous
P.O. Box 4245
St. Paul, MN 55104
612-647-9712

Founded 1971. Members share experiences, hopes, and strengths using the twelve-step program to gain better emotional health. Correspondence program for those who cannot attend local meetings. Chapter development guidelines available.

National Foundation for Depressive Illness
P.O. Box 2257
New York, NY 10016
800-239-1295

An informational service that provides a recorded message of the clear warning signs of depression and manic-depression, and instructions on how to get help and further information. For a bibliography and referral list of physicians and support groups in your area, send $5 and a self-addressed, stamped business-size envelope with 98 cents postage.

Mood Disorders Support Group, Inc.
PO. Box 1747
Madison Square Station
New York, NY 10159
212-533-MDSG

Founded 1981. Provides support and education for people with manic-depression or depression and their families and friends. Guest lectures, newsletter, rap groups, assistance in starting groups.

APPENDIX D:
Other Resources/Web Sites

American Psychiatric Association
1400 K Street, N.W.
Washington, DC 20005
phone: 202-682-6325
fax: 202-682-6255

American Psychological Association
750 First St., N.E.
Washington, DC 20002-4242
202-336-5500

Society for Light Treatment and Biological Rhythms
10200 W. 44th Avenue, Ste. 304
Wheat Ridge, CO 80033
303-424-3697

A nonprofit organization of researchers, clinicians, manufacturers, and consumers devoted to research, professional development, and clinical applications. For a "SAD Information Packet," which includes a list of research programs, send $7 plus a self-addressed, stamped envelope to Francine Butler, Ph.D., Executive Director, at the above address, or e-mail her at: sltbr@resourcenter.com.

Center for Environmental Therapeutics
P.O. Box 532
Georgetown, CO 80444
fax: 303-569-0910

*To receive a packet with information on SAD research
studies, private practitioners, and recommended reading,
send $9 along with your request to the above address.*

Winter Depression Program
Columbia-Presbyterian Medical Center,
722 W. 168th Street, Unit 50
New York, NY 10032
Conducts research into SAD and phototherapy.

Depression Awareness, Recognition, and Treatment (D/ART)
Seasonal Studies Program
5600 Fishers Lane
Rockville, MD 20857
800-421-4211
*National public and professional education program
sponsored by the National Institute of Mental Health.
D/ART's goal is the alleviation of suffering for the one in
ten American adults with depressive illness, and is based
on more than fifty years of medical research. Free
brochures available.*

National Mental Health Association
1021 Prince Street
Alexandria, VA 22314-2971
703-684-7722

Selected SAD/Depression Web Sites

http://www.columbia.edu/~mt12/

http://www.psycom.net/depression.central

http://members.aol.com/depress/children.htm

http://www.schizophrenia.com/ami/diagnosis/depress.html

http://www.nimh.nih.gov/newdart/gen_fact.htm

APPENDIX E:
Further Reading

If You Think You Have Depression, by Roger Granet, M.D., and Robin Levinson (Dell, 1998).

Fight the Winter Blues: Don't Be Sad: Your Guide to Conquering Seasonal Affective Disorder, by Celeste A. Peters (Script Publishing Inc., 1994).

Winter Blues: Seasonal Affective Disorder: What it is and how to overcome it, by Dr. Norman Rosenthal (Guilford Press, 1993).

Seasonal Affective Disorder, by Angela Smyth (HarperCollins, 1991).

Winter Depression, by Angela Smyth (Unwin Paperbacks, London, 1990).

The Light Book, by Jane Wegscheider Hyman (Ballantine Books, 1990).

INDEX